T0161298

MENDES I

PLATE I

The Great Naos of Mendes at Tell el Rubʻa in 1964

The Brooklyn Museum
and
The Institute of Fine Arts of New York University

MENDES I

Robert K. Holz, David Stieglitz, Donald P. Hansen,
and
Edward Ochsenschlager

Edited by
Emma Swan Hall and Bernard V. Bothmer

AMERICAN RESEARCH CENTER IN EGYPT
CAIRO
1980

The American Research Center in Egypt gratefully acknowledges the substantial financial contribution of the Smithsonian Institution, Washington, D.C., as well as that of a number of friends, towards the production and publication of this volume.

MENDES II
by Herman De Meulenaere and Pierre MacKay
appeared in 1976 and may be obtained from the publishers:

Aris & Phillips Ltd.
Warminster, Wilts., England

DESIGNED BY BERT CLARKE AND THOMAS WHITRIDGE
COMPOSED IN ENGLISH MONOTYPE BEMBO
PRINTED BY A. COLISH, INC., MOUNT VERNON, NEW YORK
ISBN 0-936770-02-3

CONTENTS

EDITORIAL PREFACE

"Je me suis changé en bouc de Mendès et j'ai couché avec la splendide mère
pour qu'elle donne le jour à ton être."
J. Lacarrière, *Hérodote et la découverte de la terre* (Paris, 1968), p. 111.

On a memorable day in May, 1956, Jean Yoyotte, Alexander Badawy, H. W. Müller, William K. Simpson and B. V. Bothmer visited Mendes for the first time and stood in awe, facing the Great Naos, the largest ever carved in ancient Egypt.

Most Egyptologists have heard that there was once a great site which Herodotus called "Mendes" and that there were *tells* or *koms* in the Delta marking the places where a temple or town had stood in antiquity. But nothing in the teachings of our archaeological mentors had prepared us for this overwhelming sight: the long hill, at first appearing so low in the flat landscape, the gradual rise in terrain, the view of the remains of the gigantic Enclosure Wall and finally the height of the massive Tell itself when one had scaled it and gazed over the rich landscape, far out to the distant horizon.

Later during that memorable day, the first visit to the South Kom was equally impressive—acres and acres of house ruins which, when first seen from the rise behind the village of Kafr el Amir, looked as if they had only recently been swept by a great fire. One could hardly imagine at that moment how, little more than a century ago, this enormous Tell had been reduced by one half through the removal of hundreds of thousands of cubic yards of *sebakh* on an organized scale, *sebakh*—fertilized by a thousand years of occupation in antiquity—which now enriched the verdant fields for miles around.

Mendes, like Memphis, is a geographical term which can be applied to a specific site as well as to an entire region. The Mendesian Nome, the Mendesian Branch of the Nile, are both named after the place which Herodotus, quoting Pindar, called "Mendes" in Greek.

Situated about ninety miles north of Cairo, between the modern towns of es-Simbillâwein and Mansurah, Mendes is the last major archaeological site in the Egyptian Delta to have remained largely unexplored. The town has a long history. We cannot at this time state when it was first settled, since the lowest levels have yet to be excavated, but antiquities from the early Old Kingdom (ca. 2700 B.C.) have been found, and the place was occupied well into the Christian era (ca. A.D. 800). During Dynasty XXIX, in the fourth century B.C., Mendes became the capital of Egypt, an honor shared by few other towns. It covers an area of about four hundred and seventy-five acres and is still, in many places, about thirty feet above the present level of cultivation surrounding it. In antiquity, one of the branches of the Nile passed close by the western side of Mendes.

Mendes is characterized by two *koms* or *tells*, man-made hillocks created by successive habitation and building levels over the ages. The North Kom, Tell el Rub'a, contains the remains of Mendes from the Pharaonic Period; the South Kom, Tell Timai, consists of impressive remains of buildings from the Ptolemaic and Roman Periods and was called Thmuis. Today the name "Mendes" has two meanings. On the one hand it designates Tell el Rub'a as distinct from Tell Timai; on the other hand, it is the name of the site as a whole, comprising both Koms.

In antiquity, Mendes was dedicated to a triad whose chief deity was the ram-headed god Banebdjed, known to Classical authors as the "Ram of Mendes." His consort, identified with a dolphin-like fish, was called Hatmehit, "she-who-is-at-the-head-of-the-fishes." The child Horus was their offspring. On the North Kom, Tell el Rub'a, there are still to be seen over thirty stone sarcophagi in which the sacred rams of Mendes were buried.

The ram was of a species with extended horns, *ovis longipes palaeoaegyptus* which, while it continued to be represented as the local deity, was not found in Egypt after the Middle Kingdom (ca. 2000 B.C.). From the Persian Period (after 525 B.C.), according to Herodotus, a he-goat was considered the sacred animal of Mendes.

The Egyptian origin of the Greek name, "Mendes," has been convincingly explained by Hermann Kees.[1] Whether Pindar (518–438 B.C.) or Herodotus (485–425 B.C.) mentions

1. H. Kees, in *RE* XV (1932), cols. 783–84 (*Mendes* II, Pp. 148–51).

Mendes first is hard to decide. It was the Greek misunderstanding of "Ram, Lord of Djedet," the ancient Egyptian "Banebdjed" which led to the Greek "Mendes," Djedet being the town's ancient Egyptian name. Still, scholars to this day prefer to call Mendes by its Greek name.

The origin of the name "Thmuis" has been discussed by Jean Yoyotte.[2] Briefly, he explains its meaning as "le terrain neuf." It is first mentioned by Josephus (A.D. 37–95), then in Ptolemy's *Geography* (ca. A.D. 150); appears so on medieval maps, and even on modern maps after the Napoleonic Expedition (1798–1801), instead of Mendes. Cartographers, until 1875, unaware that the two sites were adjoining, were apt to use the name "Mendes" for other sites to the north (Plates 5 to 11). Timai el Amdid, the town nearest the Koms, combines the two names, Mendes and Thmuis, in reverse order (*Mendes* II, p. 9).

The two Koms which constitute Mendes are, as mentioned above, Tell el Rub'a and Tell Timai. Tell el Rub'a takes its name from the nearby village of El Rub'a, while Tell Timai is what an Arab geographer called "the mound of the new land," confirming Yoyotte's interpretation of the name. What Yoyotte describes as "l'espace entre les deux buttes . . . parcouru par un canal ancien qui suit, selon toute vraisemblance, le tracé d'un antique bras du Nil" contradicts the view that originally there was only one large Kom.[3] Nevertheless, the El Shiwan Canal dividing them today does not appear on maps until 1888 (Plate 12-e).

In this volume, Mendes and Thmuis are introduced by Mr. Holz in their cartographical and geographical aspects. Mr. Stieglitz will relate how the most recent topographical map of the sites was made. Mr. Hansen and Mr. Ochsenschlager describe the place as it looks now.

Before the excavations by The Brooklyn Museum–New York University Expedition, it was not known that the history of the site went back to Early Dynastic times. Nor was it known that the Great Naos, a colossal granite shrine, twenty-one feet tall, standing in its original position since the time of King Amasis and representing the highest point in the Delta, once shared the sanctuary space with three other naoi of equal size.

It should perhaps be added that the Great Naos does not face True North, but deviates from it by a little more than 21° East. Therefore, the direction in which it faces, as also the great Enclosure Wall, has been called Northnortheast instead of North. All indications on the Plates have been so designated.

During the first season of 1964, excavations were conducted by The Brooklyn Museum and the Institute of Fine Arts, New York University, with the assistance of the Detroit Institute of Arts and the Oriental Institute of the University of Chicago.

Since its inception, the Mendes Expedition has been sponsored locally by the American Research Center in Egypt, with the cooperation of the Department of Egyptian Antiquities in Cairo, now called the Organisation of Egyptian Antiquities.

In that first season, excavations were conducted in an area containing burials from the Old Kingdom, which were covered over by private houses and by part of the temple. This grouping is very unusual for an excavation site in Egypt. A pottery sequence was established by which subsequent examples could be compared and dated.

The seasons of 1965 and 1966 concentrated mainly on the site of the Great Naos. Excavations revealed that this area originally contained four such shrines, arranged in a square on a platform. The excavators uncovered intact, under the four corners of the platform once bearing the Great Naos and its companions, the foundation deposits of King Amasis (570–526 B.C.) of Dynasty XXVI. His name also appears on the Great Naos.

To the northwest of the Naos three mudbrick mastabas, tombs dating from the First Intermediate Period (2180–1990 B.C.), were uncovered. Some of them were provided with limestone revetments inscribed in hieroglyphs. From these blocks the name of Ba-kherepu was recovered.

Because of the 1967 War, the Expedition was unable to continue its activities since, for reasons of security, the Delta was closed to all archaeologists.

Work was resumed at Mendes in 1976. At that time Brooklyn College joined The Brooklyn Museum and the Institute of Fine Arts at the site. The staff from Brooklyn College centered its work at the South Kom, Tell Timai. Excavations on the North Kom were resumed in the area of the mastabas of the Old Kingdom.

In the summer of 1977, work was conducted in three major areas. The mastaba complex revealed a large burial belonging to a woman of means. Her funerary equipment consisted of a bronze mirror, alabaster vessels, and several sheets of gold which had been placed over her body.

A second site was explored for the first time in the area around the so-called sarcophagus of King Nepherites. Here the excavators uncovered a cache of statues dated to the Late Period, several of which bear hieroglyphic inscriptions with the names of people known from other sources as having been active in Mendes, Heliopolis, and Saft el Henna.

Finally, the area known locally as Kom el 'Izam, the "Mound of Bones," was investigated. A remarkable hoard of Hellenistic pottery vessels was found. Almost every vessel was intact, and some bore fine floral motifs related to examples in Alexandria.

The commitment to scholarship has been maintained from the beginning, through preliminary reports on the excavations, which have appeared in the *Journal* and *Newsletter of the American Research Center* and in the *Brooklyn Museum Annual*. *Mendes* II, the first of the volumes to appear, deals with the his-

---

2. *Mendes* II, Pp. 168–69; J. Yoyotte, in *GLECS* 8 (1961), pp. 100–01, and 9 (1962), pp. 5–9.
3. Ibid. 9 (1962), p. 7; also O. Toussoun, in *MIE* 8 (1925), p. 178. For a contrary view, see below, P. 25.

tory of the site, *Mendes* I with its geographical and topographical aspects.

It is amazing how, to this day, the ravages of the *sebbakhin* have not yet succeeded in reducing the entire Delta landscape to agricultural level. Foucart[4] stated in 1901 that the smaller *tells* of the Delta had completely disappeared and that most of those of middling size were being destroyed. He added that the very large *tells*, among which he lists Tell Timai, would still last for a number of years. He continues: "Mais, même pour ceux-ci il faut bien se persuader que l'exploitation croissante, soit pour le sébakh, soit pour les briques, arrivera à les effacer."

In 1907, a report on the Delta Inspectorate[5] states:

M. Edgar maintient l'ordre avec vigueur dans cet inspectorat, et les opérations du sébakh ainsi que la surveillance des tells s'y poursuivent régulièrement; sur deux points toutefois, dans le Béhéra et dans la Dakahliéh, les empiètements se produisent journellement malgré nos efforts. Les tribunaux ont beau reconnaître nos droits, l'autorité administrative se montre impuissante à faire exécuter les jugements, et, presque partout, les terrains qui nous été rendus une année nous sont soustraits l'année suivante en dépit de notre surveillance: il faut tout recommencer. En résumé, d'un bout à l'autre de l'Egypte, la portion du domaine de l'État dont la garde nous a été confiée est attaquée et diminue sans que, ni les lois, ni la coutume, ni l'esprit général de la population, nous aident à la défendre efficacement.

Also, Labib Habachi, Egypt's most renowned scholar in the ancient field, added in 1943,[6] an introductory note to his "Sais and its Monuments," warning about the activities of the *sebbakhin*, and as recently as 1966, H. W. Müller[7] deplored in print that the leveling off of the ancient *koms* of the Delta continued, even on land belonging to the Department of Antiquities.

We owe a debt of gratitude to Labib Habachi for having consistently, throughout a long career, stressed the importance of the Delta as a vital part of ancient Egypt and the source for much of its history and antiquities. The same honor goes to Jean Yoyotte and, more recently, to Manfred Bietak, because even today it is amazing and to a certain extent appalling how visitors to Egypt, laymen as well as scholars, ignore the Delta. This neglect, which is one of the major reasons for the despoliation of the ancient *tells* and *koms*, also puzzled Flinders Petrie who, as early as 1886, stated:[8]

There are hundreds of English travellers who are familiar with Upper Egypt and its towns; but it would be easier to find anyone to give a scientific account of the sources of the Nile, than one who could give an archaeological account of the remains thickly scattered about its mouths.

In this connection it is well worth quoting Jean de Rougé who wrote[9] in 1891:

4. G. Foucart, in *ASAE* 2 (1901), p. 50.
5. *Rapport sur la Marche du Service des Antiquités 1899–1910*, p. 227.
6. L. Habachi, in *ASAE* 42 (1943), pp. 369–370.
7. H. W. Müller, *Bericht über im März/April 1966 in das östliche Nildelta unternommene Erkundungsfahrten* (Munich, 1966), pp. 10–11.
8. W. M. Flinders Petrie, *Naukratis* I = EEF *Memoirs* III (London, 1886), p. 1.
9. J. de Rougé, *Géographie ancienne de la Basse-Egypte* (Paris, 1891), p. xi.

Dans la Basse-Egypte les fouilles ont été entreprises de tout temps avec infiniment moins d'ardeur et surtout avec moins de suite que dans le reste de la vallée du Nil: la difficulté des recherches y entraîne des dépenses beaucoup plus considérables, car les monuments y sont bien plus profondément enfouis: les cités et les temples, ruinés par les invasions successives dont la Basse-Egypte eut toujours a supporter les premières fureurs, ont vu succéder des périodes alternatives de splendeur et de décadence: le limon du Nil est venu à son tour recouvrir les assises les plus anciennes quand il n'a pas fait disparaître jusqu'au souvenir de la cité elle-même. Et cependant les ruines sont là, sous la couche épaisse, attendant le fouilleur qui viendra arracher leurs trésors historiques.

One reason for the long delay of excavations in the Delta probably has to do with the building of the Aswan Dam in the south, which was twice raised, and more recently with the construction of the much larger High Dam. Each time miles of land with a history and of archaeological interest were flooded, with the result that scholars studied and recorded the Nile Valley to the south of Aswan, now all of it under water, more diligently than any other part of the country.

Another reason why most scholars shunned excavating in the Delta is that they feared the relatively high subsoil water level and, as Labib Habachi[10] explained in 1943, "most of the ancient sites are below the level of the subsoil water." Fortunately for Mendes though, which consists of two quite high mounds, this problem has hardly come up.

Unfortunately, except for military purposes, and apart from the views shown on Plates 28 and 36, the Delta has never been adequately surveyed from the air. The Editors have been unable to obtain detailed air views, not only of Mendes, but also of the changes in landscape affecting the Delta as a whole over the last fifty years. Still, an eminent scholar of Egyptian archaeology, Reginald Engelbach (1888–1946), at one time Keeper of the Egyptian Museum in Cairo, wrote[11] as early as 1929:

The air-photographs most urgently needed are undoubtedly those of the Delta 'tells'. A *tell* is the result of the construction, for thousands of years, of mud-brick houses on the ruins of their predecessors. In some, the process still continues, while others, such as Tell Fara'în, the ancient Buto, stand grim and deserted, covering hundreds of acres and rising to a height of 60 feet or more above the surrounding fields.

Very little excavation has been carried out on the Delta *tells*, though in ancient times some of them were towns as important and wealthy as the better known sites of Upper Egypt. The soil-level is many metres higher than it was in Pharaonic times, and if one excavates on the present soil-level it is no unusual thing to find that the objects discovered are of Ptolemaic date or even later. To excavate a *tell* for early remains would mean descending deep below water level by the use of powerful pumps, a costly and by no means healthy procedure. The British School of Archaeology in Egypt, under Sir Flinders Petrie, carried out such excavations in a mild way for several seasons in the Ptah Temple of Memphis, and the statuary and sculptures found some 2 metres below subsoil water-level well repaid the expense incurred. If a part of Buto, for example, were excavated level by

10. L. Habachi, op. cit., p. 369.
11. R. Engelbach, in *Antiquity, A Quarterly Review of Archaeology* 3 (1929), p. 472.

level, objects of outstanding interest would surely come to light, though possibly only after several years of barren work.

Most of the old towns were surrounded by huge brick walls, a thickness of forty feet being common. Though the walls are being steadily destroyed by the *fellahin* for use as manure for their crops, many are still traceable, those of Mendes (Tell Tmai) still rising high above the level of the ruined city. Here the temple wall can also clearly be followed. It is in this connexion that an air-survey is so urgently needed. Though the walls of Athribis (Benha), Saïs (Sâ al-Hagar), and Heliopolis have been destroyed to such an extent that it is doubtful whether air-photographs would even reveal their course, those of Xois, Tanis, Mendes and Buto and a dozen less important sites would well repay the time expended on an air-survey.

Flying-time is not cheap for a civilian enterprise and the R.A.F. has many activities. I have suggested, however, to those in command, the possibility of permitting observers who are out practising air-photography to take as their subject the Delta tells. I have also furnished indications showing the position of those which are of the greatest interest. I am certain that had I done this a year ago my Department would be in possession of photographs of most of them.

The War of 1967 and its aftermath have, of course, done a good deal of additional damage to the ancient sites of the Delta, but the leveling process continues on land that contains a vital part of Egypt's ancient history.

"Mendes House" was built in 1964 for the personnel of the excavation. The equipment includes a generator for electricity, a water tower, storage and laboratory facilities, and living quarters for a dozen archaeologists and their household staff. The funds for equipment and building were generously provided by the Friends of Mendes, a group whose donations for this purpose were made to the Department of Egyptian and Classical Art. The Friends of Mendes also donated the hard currency necessary to begin the excavations at Mendes. Through 1978 the Foreign Currency Program of the Smithsonian Institution has provided local currency for the transportation of the staff, for daily expenses and the wages of the labor force.

For assistance with the maps in this volume the Editors wish to thank in particular Mr. and Mrs. J. J. Clère, the late Mr. Serge Sauneron, Mr. T.G.H. James, Mr. John Carswell, Mr. Jean Yoyotte, and the following institutions: in Cairo, the Société Géographique and the Institut Français d'Archéologie Orientale; in London, the Trustees of the British Museum; in Paris, the Archives des Cartes at the Château de Vincennes, the Bibliothèque Nationale, and the Collège de France; in Rome, the Vatican Library; in the United States, the Harvard College Library in Cambridge, the Library of Congress in Washington, D.C., and in New York City, the New-York Historical Society, the American Geographical Society, the New York Public Library, the library of the United Nations, and last but not least, the Wilbour Library of Egyptology at The Brooklyn Museum.

Books on which the Editors have particularly relied for reference are the Napoleonic Expedition's *Description de l'Egypte* (Second ed., published by Panckoucke [Paris, 1821–

1829], to which page numbers given in the text refer); Youssouf Kamal's invaluable volumes of the *Monumenta Cartographica Africae et Aegypti* (Cairo, 1926–1951), and John Ball's *Egypt in the Classical Geographers* (Cairo, 1949).

Two monuments, sometimes stated to have been found at Tell el Rub'a, are not listed in *Mendes* II (pp. 191 ff.) among the finds from Mendes. They are the naos of Apries in Cairo (CG 70008) and a torso of Nectanebo I, also in Cairo (JE 38167). The inscriptions on both objects name *Thoth of Rehuy* and they undoubtedly came originally from that site, modern El Baqliya, 11 km. west of Mendes. The confusion has arisen because one of the *koms* of El Baqliya was at one time also named Tell el Rub'a.[12]

A number of personalities from Mendes, not yet encountered at the site but found in other parts of the Nile Valley, can be identified by their worship of Mendesian deities. For instance, a certain Pyiay, "Fan Bearer on the Right of the King," is shown on a pilaster in the southern temple at Buhen, worshiping the anthropomorphic Ba-neb-djed with ram's head, in a relief dated to Year 3 of Merenptah.[13]

Being well aware that nothing is perfect, we realize that *Mendes* II has certain faults and that a number of volumes have been published since it appeared which refer to the site and to what has been found there.

Inevitably, since the plates for this volume were made up, we found yet another map in color of the Mendes region on which Tell el Rub'a and Tell Timai appear: A. Boinet, *Géographie économique et administrative de l'Egypte I: Basse Egypte* (Cairo, 1902), map following p. 378. Boinet also lists the "Village of Kafr el Amir Abdallah," which then had a population of 341 (p. 392); the "Village Rob' (el)," with a population of 916 (p. 401), and the "Village Temai el Amdid," with a population of 2007 (p. 406). The omission of this reference is even more ironic, since Pierre McKay cites it on Page 11 of *Mendes* II.

An important discovery, largely thanks to Lewis McNaught of the British Museum, is the identity of yet another amateur who excavated at Tell Timai. Frank Rattigan, an officer of the British Foreign Service, in his *Diversions of a Diplomat* (London, 1924), pp. 100–103, relates how in 1912 he obtained a permit and uncovered "a Roman villa." With his own hands he bared the floor and found "no less than three mosaics in practically unspoiled condition."

Since **161**[14] (*Mendes* II, p. 212) was sent to Alexandria in 1912 and most of the other mosaics in 1923 and 1924, it is impossible to tell which ones he discovered. Perhaps some day additional material will be found which gives a further clue to the provenance of some of these mosaics.

Since 1975 we have, of course, the splendid publications of

---

12. L. Habachi, in *ASAE* 53 (1956), pp. 444 and 450.

13. R. Caminos, *The New Kingdom Temples of Buhen* I (1974) = *Arch.-Survey of Egypt, Memoir* 33, pp. 28–29, pls. 31–33.

14. Numbers in bold face refer to the List of Objects in *Mendes* II, Pp. 191–217.

the *Tell el-Dab'a* series by Manfred Bietak, of which three parts have already appeared. Throughout volume II he refers to Mendes, the Nome of Mendes, and the Mendesian branch of the Nile.[15] Full of admiration for his scholarship, we gladly acknowledge that his research in many ways extends far beyond ours.

It should be remembered that in the course of excavation the photographic survey of the site has not always been maintained as consistently as we would like, and the views given on

15. M. Bietak, *Tell el-Dab'a* II (Vienna, 1975), passim.

Plates 27–40 will be enlarged in a future volume of this series. Our ancient Egyptian dates are based on those of J. von Beckerath, *Abriss der Geschichte des alten Ägypten* (Munich and Vienna, 1971).

Pages, Plates and Figures printed with a capital letter refer to those in the *Mendes* volumes. A list of Addenda and Errata for *Mendes* II may be found on Pages 79–81 of this volume. The authors and editors would welcome information on any important cartographical and geographical source material which they have overlooked.

LIST OF PLATES

Chapter I. *The Cartography of Mendes*

While the title of each map is given, in most instances the area shown includes only the Mendes-Thmuis site. Following the title, the source appears in smaller type. The right hand columns give the place and date of publication, when known, followed by a reference to volume, fascicule and folio number in Y. Kamal, *Monumenta Cartographica Africae et Aegypti* I–V (Cairo, 1926–1951).

Chapter IV. *Mendes Today*

The Great Naos does not face True North but deviates from it by a little more than 21° East. Therefore the direction in which it faces, as also the great Enclosure Wall, is called Northnortheast instead of North; all indications on the plates have been so designated.

BIBLIOGRAPHY AND ABBREVIATIONS

J. B. B. d'Anville, *Mémoire sur l'Egypte ancienne et moderne* (Paris, 1766)

ASAE   *Annales du Service des Antiquités de l'Egypte*

M. Avi-Yonah, *The Madaba Mosaic Map* (Jerusalem, 1954)

J. Ball, *Egypt in the Classical Geographers* (Cairo, 1942)

M. Bietak, *Tell el-Dab'a* II (Vienna, 1975)

L. A. Brown, *The Story of Maps* (Boston, 1949)

H. K. Brugsch, *L'exode et les monuments égyptiens* (Leipzig, 1875)

H. K. Brugsch, *A History of Egypt* (London, 1875)

Bulletin de la Société [Royale]de Géographie d'Egypte

The Cairo Scientific Journal

CAH   *Cambridge Ancient History*, third ed. (Cambridge, 1970–1973)

W. R. Dawson and E. P. Uphill, *Who Was Who in Egyptology* (London, 1972)

Description   France. Commission des Monuments d'Egypte, *Description de l'Egypte*, second ed. (Paris, 1821–1829)

EEF   Egypt Exploration Fund

Egypt. Ministry of Finance, Survey Department, *A List of Maps, Plans and Publications Published up to 31st December 1907* (Cairo, 1908)

Egypt. Ministry of War and Marine, Meteorological Department, Climate Section, *Climatological Normal for Egypt* (Cairo, 1950)

"Extrait du *Journal officiel* du Gouvernement égyptien du Samedi 12 février 1910."

J. Fischer, S.J., *Claudii Ptolemaei Geographiae Codex Urbinas Graecus 82* I (Leipzig, 1932)

A. Fontaine, *Monographe cartographique de l'Isthme de Suez* II (Cairo, 1955)

A. Gayet, *Itinéraire illustré de la Haute Egypte* (Paris, [1893])

Géographie (Paris)

GLECS   *Comptes rendus du groupe linguistique d'études chamito-sémitiques*

W. Hamilton, *Aegyptiaca* (London, 1809)

J. C. Herold, *Bonaparte in Egypt* (New York, 1962)

E. Honigmann, *Trois mémoires posthumes d'histoire et de géographie de l'Orient chrétien* (Brussels, 1961)

Journal of the Royal Asiatic Society

Y. Kamal, *Monumenta Cartographica Africae et Aegypti* I (Cairo, 1926), II,1 (1928), III,1–4 (1930–1934)

Al-Kindi, *The Governors and Judges of Egypt*, transl. A. R. Guest (Leiden, 1912)

C. R. Lepsius, *Denkmaeler* I (Berlin, 1859)

M. Le Quien, *Oriens Christianus* II (Paris, 1740)

Linant de Bellefonds, *Mémoire sur les principaux travaux d'utilité publique executés en Egypte* (Paris, 1872–73)

H. Lorin, *Bibliographie géographique de l'Egypte* (Cairo, 1928)

J. Mazuel, *L'oeuvre géographique de Linant de Bellefonds* (Cairo, 1937).

MDIK   *Mitteilungen des Deutschen Archäologischen Instituts, Abteilung Kairo*

ME   *Mendes Expedition*

J. F. Michaud, *Correspondence d'Orient* VI (Paris, 1831)

MIE   *Mémoires présentés à l'Institut d'Egypte*

O. Neugebauer, *The Exact Sciences in Antiquity* (Providence, 1957)

RE   *Revue Egyptologique*

J. Rennell, *The Geographical System of Herodotus* II (London, 1830)

Science (Washington, D.C.)

A. Strahler, *Physical Geography* (New York, 1960)

V. and G. Täckholm, *The Flora of Egypt* I (Cairo, 1941), III (1954)

C. W. Thornwaite Associates, *Average Climatic Water Balance Data of the Continents*, Part I, *Africa* XV (Centerton, N.J., 1962)

O. Toussoun, *La géographie de l'Egypte à l'époque arabe* = *Mémoires de la Societé Royale de Géographie d'Egypte* VIII, 2, 3 (1928, 1936)

O. Toussoun, *Mémoires sur les anciennes branches du Nil, époque ancienne* = *MIE* IV (Cairo, 1922)

ZDPV   *Zeitschrift des Deutschen Palästina-Vereins*

J. H. Zumberge, *Elements of Geology* (New York, 1963)

MENDES I

I

THE CARTOGRAPHY OF MENDES

By ROBERT K. HOLZ[1]

Historical Summary

Map making began in the great riverine valleys of the Middle East. The earliest maps are those which the Babylonians drew on clay. The oldest known map, found at Nuzi near Kirkuk in northern Mesopotamia, dates from 2400–2200 B.C.[2]

The oldest Egyptian map is a papyrus from Gebelein in the Turin Museum (nos. Cat. 1879, 1899, 1969) of the gold mines in the region of the Wadi Hammamat in the eastern desert, between Koptos and the Red Sea. It is datable to the reign of Ramesses IV in Dynasty XX, around 1160 B.C.[3] Except for the imaginary "maps" of the nether world painted on coffins as early as the Middle Kingdom, no other maps of Egypt from the Pharaonic Period survive. From late Predynastic times, however, at the end of the fourth millennium, the Egyptians, motivated mainly by a desire to control inundation and irrigation and to establish a basis for land taxes, introduced practical cadastral surveys.

From the geographical descriptions of Herodotus, Strabo, and others, it has been possible to reconstruct maps of Egypt as they perceived it (Plate 2). Greek cartography was introduced after 332 B.C. when Alexander the Great came to Egypt. The only map surviving from the Graeco-Roman Period which shows Mendes-Thmuis is that of Ptolemy (Claudius Ptolemaeus, ca. A.D. 90–168), known from copies. The earliest, identifying Thmuis, are dated to the late twelfth or early thirteenth century A.D.: the *Codex Urbinas Graecus 82* in the Vatican (Plate 3-a) and an Arabic map[4] at the Monastery of Vatopedi on Mt. Athos.

Dating to A.D. 560–565, the *Madaba Mosaic Map*,[5] a mosaic of the Christian world with Greek captions, was set into the floor of a church in Jordan (Plate 3-e and -f). It is not only the earliest known Christian map, but the only extant Byzantine map. A seventeenth century copy of another early map, the so-called *Thronos Alexandrinos* (Plate 5-a), with Greek and Arabic captions, is dated between A.D. 675–703.[6] It was found in Jerusalem in 1722 and is now in the British Museum.

Early manuscript maps in Arabic do not include Mendes or Thmuis. However, *el Mandid*, *Tomay* and *Tumaiy* are mentioned in various Arabic writings from the seventh through the fourteenth century and have been identified as Thmuis on modern reconstructions of the Delta for that period.[7]

The earliest European printed maps to include Mendes-Thmuis, still based on the work of Ptolemy, are those of Abraham Ortelius in 1565 (Plate 4-b) and of Gerhard Mercator in 1578 (Plate 4-c). Map makers continued to copy them until early in the eighteenth century when, for missionary work or for purposes of trade, European travelers made frequent visits to Egypt. Some of them left descriptions of the country, and a few drew maps. Paul Lucas, searching for art treasures for Louis XIV, made a map of Egypt in 1717 (Plate 6-a), and Père Claude Sicard, a Jesuit priest visiting Coptic monasteries, made a map in 1722 (Plate 6-b). These are the first examples of modern cartography of Egypt and they both record Thmuis.

Père Sicard's map was copied until around 1750 when J. B. B. d'Anville, without ever going to Egypt, improved upon its accuracy, added more detail and especially listed more place names (Plate 6-e). D'Anville's map of Egypt dated 1765 (Plate 7-a) was used at the beginning of the Napoleonic Campaign in 1798 until the Commission du Cadastre de l'Egypte,

1. Robert K. Holz is Professor of Geography at the University of Texas. He is indebted to numerous people for reading and making suggestions at various stages in the preparation of his manuscript. Special thanks go to Professor William B. Conroy, whose constructive criticism is most valued, and to Miss Mary Kennedy who performed some of the necessary research. Her help was made possible by a grant from the University Research Institute in the Graduate School at the University of Texas.

2. Lloyd A. Brown, *The Story of Maps* (Boston, 1949), p. 33 and plate facing p. 38.

3. J. Černý, *CAH*, third ed., II (1975), ch. XXXV, p. 609.

4. Y. Kamal, *Monumenta Cartographica Africae et Aegypti* II,1 (Cairo, 1928), pp. 130, 131.

5. M. Avi-Yonah, *The Madaba Mosaic Map* (Jerusalem, 1954), p. 18.

6. E. Honigmann, "La valeur historique du 'Thronos Alexandrinos'", in *Trois mémoires posthumes d'histoire et de géographie de l'Orient chrétien* (Brussels, 1961).

7. Al-Kindi, *The Governors and Judges of Egypt* (Leiden, 1912), A. R. Guest (transl.), map; A. R. Guest, "The Delta in the Middle Ages," in *Journal of the Royal Asiatic Society*, 1912, pp. 941–980; Omar Toussoun, *Mémoire sur les anciennes branches du Nil, Epoque ancienne* = *MIE* IV (1922), ch. V; idem. *Géographie de l'Egypte à l'époque arabe* = *Mémoires de la Société Royale de Géographie d'Egypte* VIII (1926–1936). See also *Mendes* II, Pp. 7–11.

under the direction of Colonel Jacotin, drew the detailed maps which are one of the great achievements of the French Expedition to Egypt.

From its first publication in 1809, the scientific work of the Commission des Sciences et des Arts of the French Army, the *Description de l'Egypte*, attracted European scholars and adventurers to the Nile Valley. With the building of the Alexandria-Cairo railroad in 1855 and, in particular, with the opening of the Suez Canal in 1869, British and French interest in Egypt increased and new mapping projects were undertaken.

Rapid advances were made during this period in cartographical techniques and methods, so that finally only place names had to be corrected. Mendes, for instance, was located too far to the north on older maps, but after the Mendes Stela was found in 1871,[8] H. Brugsch identified the ancient town as one of the two great mounds adjoining the modern village of Timai el Amdid.

When the British occupied Egypt in 1882, they established an excellent mapping service, the Survey of Egypt, under the Ministry of Finance.

Classical Sources[9]

The best work on Egypt dealing with the geographical writings of the Classical authors is by John Ball.[10] He located the place names mentioned in Classical texts on the map of Egypt and correctly associated Thmuis with the South Kom, now called Tell Timai el Amdid, and Mendes with the North Kom, now Tell el Rub'a.

On the basis of Herodotus' account of his visit to Egypt around 450 B.C., Ball compiled a map of the lower part of the Nile Valley locating the sites which Herodotus named (Plate 2-a). Mendes and Thmuis appear as separate sites, next to each other, north and south. The Mendesian branch of the Nile, an eastern distributary[11] of the Sebennytic branch, passes close to the west of the sites which are located in the east Central Delta, in their approximate true geographical position. They are slightly to the south of the latitude of Tanis which, according to Herodotus, was situated on the Saïtic channel of the Sebennytic branch of the Nile.[12a]

In 59 B.C. Diodorus Siculus visited Egypt. He mentions both the nome and the city of Mendes, but does not refer to Thmuis. Strabo in his *Geography*, written around 24 B.C., lists ninety-nine cities and other settlements in Egypt which Ball enumerates in alphabetical order together with their modern names. Mendes occupies a place on this list, but Thmuis does not. On

the basis of Strabo's comments and list, Ball drew up another map of Lower Egypt and the Nile Delta (Plate 2-b). Mendes is shown just to the east of the Mendesian branch of the Nile, in its approximate true geographical position. Thmuis does not appear, but in its place is Diospolis, a city which in reality lay much farther to the north.

Pliny the Elder (A.D. 23–79) in his *Natural History* refers only to the Mendesian nome and the Mendesian mouth of the Nile.

Ptolemy (Claudius Ptolemaeus) was born around A.D. 90 in Upper Egypt, but spent most of his life in Alexandria. He is the first geographer known to have drawn a map of Egypt which has been transmitted to us, although only in copies. He is the most significant figure in the history of geography and cartography of the ancient world. Ptolemy's map of Lower Egypt in Ball's book (Plate 2-c) shows only Thmuis and not Mendes. The Mendesian branch of the Nile is not given, but the Busiritic branch, which is not listed by Strabo, appears to the east of the site. Ball's next map shows the true geographic positions of the places mentioned in Ptolemy (Plate 2-d). If both Strabo and Ptolemy are correct in the positions and names of the Nile branches in their time, a considerable change occurred in the Delta between the first century B.C. and the end of the first century A.D. The Mendesian distributaries, having disappeared without trace, were replaced by a more eastern stream, the Busiritic branch.[12b]

Ball compiled a list of the nomes of Upper and Lower Egypt known to Herodotus, Strabo, Pliny and Ptolemy.[13] He lists the Mendesian nome, mentioned by all four writers, and gives Mendes as its principal town with the modern name of *Tell el-Rub'a*. He adds that Mendes was later known as Thmuis, with the modern name *Tell Timai el-Amdid*. Then he lists the Thmuite nome, mentioned only by Herodotus, with *Thmuis* (*Tell Timai el-Amdid*) as its principal town.

Thumuis (Thmuis) occurs in the *Itinerarium Provinciarum Antonini Augusti*, the Antonine Itinerary, which dates from the time of Diocletian, around A.D. 300.[14] In this document *Thumuis* is located twenty-two Roman miles from *Pelusio* (Pelusium) on the road to Alexandria, via Tanis and Cynopolis (Abusir Bana).

The *Notitia Dignitatum et Administrationum omnium tam civilium quam militarium*, dating from the reign of Valentinian III (A.D. 425–455),[15] lists *Thmou* (Thmuis) as a Roman military garrison.[16]

Around A.D. 527 Stephanus of Byzantium compiled a geographical dictionary in Greek, said to have consisted of sixty volumes. He collected place names and their locations from the writings of numerous of his predecessors and lists both Mendes and Thmuis.[17]

8. *Mendes* II, Pp. 173–77, and *List of Objects* III, Pp. 205–06. Numbers given in boldface type refer throughout *Mendes* I and II to the objects from Mendes-Thmuis listed in *Mendes* II, Pp. 191–219.

9. See also *Mendes* II, Chapter I, Pp. 1–4.

10. John Ball, *Egypt in the Classical Geographers* (Cairo, 1942).

11. During the inundation, alluvium deposited in the Delta causes the river to divide around it into two or more streams. As these streams subdivide further they create a triangle or fan-shaped area interlaced by a network of channels called distributaries.

12a. Ball, op. cit. pp. 26–27.

12b. Ibid., p. 129.

13. Ibid., pp. 122–123.

14. Ibid., p. 138.

15. Ibid., p. 160.

16. Ibid., p. 162.

17. Ibid., pp. 167, 172, 175.

In his *Synecdemus* or Travel Companion, about A.D. 535, the grammarian Hierocles lists *Thmues* (Thmuis) as one of the thirteen towns of the Eparchy of the First Augusta, a Roman designation for the northeastern part of the Delta.[18]

In his *Description of the Roman World*, compiled in about A.D. 606, George of Cyprus lists the dioceses of Egypt (Plate 2-e). *Thmuis* is located in Eparchy 'A' of *Augustamnica*, while Mendes is not mentioned.[19] This work may have been used, at least in part, for the *Thronos Alexandrinos* list by an anonymous author, accompanying a seventh century map of Egypt which the Reverend Richard Pococke found in Jerusalem in 1722, discussed below.[20] George of Cyprus' work takes us to within thirty-three years of the Arab Conquest of Egypt.

From the Middle Ages to Modern Times

Throughout the Middle Ages, Ptolemy's *Geography* was largely unknown in the West, although Arabic cartographers such as Idrisi (born A.D. 1100) must have had access to copies of it. This is evident from the numerous maps of Egypt already beginning to appear in the eleventh century,[21] some of which are clearly based on Ptolemy. None, however, locate the ruins of Mendes-Thmuis.

Pressure from Islam may have brought learned refugees with copies of Ptolemy's maps from Byzantium to the West. The earliest version of his map of Egypt is the so-called *Codex Urbinas Graecus 82* in the Vatican (Plate 3-a), which was drawn at the end of the twelfth or the beginning of the thirteenth century.[22] This map locates Thmuis. Another mediaeval version of Ptolemy's map of Egypt is the *Codex Athos Graecus* in Greek and Arabic, which Father Fischer has dated to the beginning of the fourteenth century.[23] The first copy with Latin captions derived from the *Codex Urbinas Graecus 82* is the *Codex Vaticanus Latinus 5698* (Plate 3-b) datable to the early fifteenth century.[24]

Another lost document of antiquity which was copied by a monk of Colmar in 1265 is chronologically later than Ptolemy's original map of Egypt, but earlier than any of the known copies. It is an *itinerarium scriptum*, or road map, of the Roman Empire. The copy is known as the *Tabula Peutingeriana*, named after Conrad Peutinger (1465–1547) of Augsburg, who acquired it. The map is drawn on a long parchment strip. Segmentum VIII,4 (Plate 3-c and -d) shows the section illustrating the Delta. Thmuis appears as *TM* near the seashore in the north. Ortelius read the letter to the right, on the other side of the Nile branch, taking "u" for *TMu* or Thmuis. However,

it may merely be an abbreviation of "urbis." In the middle of the eighteenth century, a site near the sea was once again chosen for Thmuis on a few English and French maps (Plate 7-c and -d).

The Madaba Mosaic Map of A.D. 560–565 (Plate 3-e and -f) is earlier than any of these copies. It has recently been republished by Professor Avi-Yonah[25] who, however, merely mentions Thmuis on a list.[26] On this floor map, south faces the altar, and the inscriptions are directed toward the observer who faces east as he enters the church. Only a portion of the Egyptian Delta is preserved.

A great Egyptian student of Arabic cartography and geography, the late Prince Omar Toussoun (1872–1944), reconstructed from the writings of Arab geographers a series of maps locating places in the Delta, among them *Tomay* (Thmuis) (Plate 4-a). Because the site was virtually uninhabited since before the Arab conquest, no original Arabic map showing Thmuis has been found.[27]

In the sixteenth century two of the great figures in the history of cartography were contemporaries and friends: Mercator (Gerhard Kremer, 1512–1594) and Ortelius (Abraham Ortel, 1527–1598). Ortelius was born in Antwerp and at the age of twenty joined the Guild of St. Luke as an illuminator of maps. In 1564, when he was thirty-seven, he published his first map, a map of the world in eight sheets. In 1565 he published *Aegyptus Antiquus*, a map of Egypt in two sheets, which was largely derived from Ptolemy, with the addition of some new information (Plate 4-b). It shows Thmuis and also the Mendesian branch of the Nile. In 1578, his great friend Mercator at the age of sixty-six made a map of Egypt which was printed in Cologne (Plate 4-c). Since the Butic River does not appear on Ptolemy's map, Ortelius' earliest map of Egypt does not show it. Mercator, however, included it on his *Aegyptus Inferior*. He probably conjectured the Butic River from his study of Ptolemy's writings where it is described in some detail.[28] Undoubtedly Mercator influenced Ortelius who inserted the Butic River on subsequent maps of Egypt.

Since this River no longer existed in the sixteenth century, it is ironical that, by omitting it on his first map of Egypt in 1565 (Plate 4-b), Ortelius more truly reflected the state of the Delta at that time. A second map which Ortelius published in 1584 (Plate 4-d) and a third in 1595 also include a line representing the Butic River. On both of these maps the Nile Delta is rendered in far more detail. The map of 1584 is the first map on record to attempt to locate *Mendes* in the *Mendesius Nomus*. Separated by the Butic River, it appears far to the north of *Thmuis* in the *Thmuites Nomus* and, thus misplaced, remained on maps for the next four hundred years.

Richard Pococke (1704–1765) acquired in Jerusalem in 1722

18. Ibid., p. 165.

19. Ibid., p. 177.

20. Pp. 5–6; Plate 5-a.

21. Y. Kamal, *Monumenta Cartographica Africae et Aegypti* III,1–4 (Cairo, 1930–1934).

22. J. Fischer, S.J., *Claudii Ptolemaei Geographiae Codex Urbinas Graecus 82*, I (Leipzig, 1932), p. 221, and see Note 4 above.

23. Ibid., p. 237.

24. Ibid., p. 290.

25. M. Avi-Yonah, *The Madaba Mosaic Map* (Jerusalem, 1954).

26. Ibid., p. 76.

27. *Mendes* II, P. 6.

28. J. Ball, *Egypt in the Classical Geographers* (Cairo, 1942), p. 129.

a copy of the often-cited map known as the *Thronos Alexandrinos* (Plate 5-a). It is now in London[29] and has been extensively studied by Ernest Honigmann[30] who dates it to the seventeenth century instead of to the seventh or eighth, as had been claimed for it hitherto.

Great cartographers of the Renaissance, such as Mercator, Ortelius, Sanson, and others, copied Ptolemy's work carefully while adding new information to it. This holds true for J.-B. Tavernier (1605–1689), who is better known for his travels in India. His map of 1640 (Plate 5-b), the first by a Frenchman to show Thmuis, again features the no-longer existing Butic River.

Actually, between the maps of Ortelius in 1584 and of Tavernier in 1640, there is another map on which *Tmuis* appears. It is by P. Bertius who, according to Kamal,[31] published it in his *Geographia Vetus* (Paris, 1630). It is, of course, merely another interpretation of Ptolemy's map.

In 1693, yet another map following Ptolemy was prepared at a scale of approximately 1 : 2,000,000. It is entitled *Les Deserts d'Egypte* (Plate 5-c) and covers the southeastern end of the Mediterranean. The map was printed in Paris by E. Michalet and depicts places supposed to have been inhabited by the *Saincts Pères*. It is in color, with many figures of people, animals, churches, monks in caves, and areas under cultivation. A crude physiographic diagramming is used to show topographic features, and non-existent landforms are liberally distributed over the countryside. Mendes does not appear, but Thmuis is shown in its approximate true geographical position.

Two other late seventeenth century maps, also based on Ptolemy's work, are entitled *Aegyptus Antiqua*. One is by Nicolas Sanson, Sieur d'Abbéville (1600–1667), who founded the French school of cartography (Plate 5-d). The other is by his pupil and son-in-law, Pierre Du Val (1619–1683) (Plate 5-e). The maps illustrated here are from editions dated respectively 1705 and probably 1710. Du Val has certainly copied Sanson's map, but shows west instead of north at the top. If Du Val's map formed part of an atlas, it would explain the 90° rotation. As on Ortelius' map *Mendes N.* is incorrectly located, and *Thmuis N.* on one map, *Themnis N.* on the other, are shown south of the Butic River.

Both Sanson and Du Val's maps are on a scale of approximately 1 : 200,000, further evidence that one was copied from the other. However, Sanson's map is in color, while Du Val's is in black and white. Both are somewhat schematic and pictorial, with a crude attempt to suggest landforms.

A *Carte de la Basse Egypte* by the famous traveler Paul Lucas (1664–1737) is dated 1717. It locates *Themaie* east of Mansurah (Plate 6-a) with a sketch of ruins which includes two standing obelisks and one which has fallen. Since Lucas never visited the site, he obviously confused it with the ruins of Tanis.

A significant event in the cartography of Egypt was the new map of Père Claude Sicard, S.J. (1677–1726), based on autopsy rather than on secondary information. It is entitled *Carte/de l'Egypte ancienne/divisée/En ses 58 Nomes ou Gouvernements. . . . /Presentée/A sa Majesté Très Chrétienne Louis XV, Roi de France et de Navarre/Par son très humble Serviteur Cl. Sicard Missionaire Jésuite en Egypte./au Caire 1722.* The original is preserved in the Archives des Cartes, Ministère de la Guerre, Château de Vincennes, Paris. The part showing the northeastern Delta is reproduced on Plate 6-b.

Sicard went to Egypt in 1707 and stayed there for almost twenty years, until he died in Cairo in 1726. It is a curious coincidence that the first European to make a map of Egypt based on his own observations should also be the first modern traveler who, in describing the Delta, includes Thmuis which he may have visited in May, 1714.

Sicard's map is the first truly modern cartographic survey of Egypt, and its accuracy as far as the Eastern Delta is concerned was hardly improved upon by the cartographers of the Napoleonic Expedition seventy-five years later. Sicard's map not only does away for good with the old Butic River; it establishes that by then, as now, there were only two branches of the Nile. Still, Sicard, under the influence of Ptolemy's map, locates with dotted lines the ancient branches of the Nile with their mouths on the Mediterranean. He places *Themuis* in its proper location in the *Mendes N.*, beside an unnamed canal which, coming from *Sebennytus* (Samannud), passes to the northwest of the site. Further north, slightly to the east of *Hermopolis*, this canal joins the *Mendesius Canalis* running from Mansurah to Lake Menzaleh and through it as a dotted line to the sea.

Sicard's map was initially copied by two cartographers to the King of France, Guillaume Delisle (1675–1726), who is said to have been the one who copied it on leather,[32] and Jean Baptiste Bourguignon d'Anville (1697–1782).[33] In his *Mémoire sur l'Egypte ancienne et moderne*,[34] d'Anville states that "LE ROI, par une faveur singulière, & qui m'imposoit le devoir d'un travail spécial sur l'Egypte, daigna me confier cette carte il y a environ trente-sept ans, & je conserve la copie très-fidèle que j'en fis alors." Therefore he must have made the copy (Plate 6-c) around 1729[35] and used it later for his own published maps of Egypt, the first of which is dated 1731 (Plate 6-d).[36]

Until the end of the eighteenth century, cartographers continued to follow Sicard, adapting d'Anville's maps, which were based on his, to their own use.

29. British Museum Add. MS. 5662.
30. See Note 6 above, P. 3.
31. Y. Kamal, *Monumenta* II,2, p. 256.

32. Thanks are extended to Mr. Roger Hervé, Conservateur, Bibliothèque Nationale, Paris, for this information. The map is listed in the Bibliothèque Nationale catalogue as Ge. C. 10070 and appears in Kamal, *Monumenta* II,4, fol. AA-30.
33. Paris, Bibliothèque Nationale, Coll. d'Anville 7804 (Kamal, op. cit., fol. AA-31).
34. J. B. B. d'Anville, *Mémoire sur l'Egypte ancienne et moderne* (Paris, 1766), p. iv.
35. Kamal gives 1722 as a date which refers, however, to Sicard's map and not to d'Anville's copy.
36. Mich. Le Quien, *Oriens Christianus* II (Paris, 1740), pp. 329–330.

Although d'Anville himself never went to Egypt, he wrote about it[37] and in 1750 produced his first map of modern Egypt, entitled *Egypte nommée dans le pays Missir* (Plate 6-e). It is a more sophisticated version of Sicard's map which he follows by placing *Temayé* in approximately its correct location. The scale of the map is about 1:1,300,000. Expression of topography on this map is very similar to that of Vaugondy, another royal cartographer and d'Anville's contemporary (Plate 7-d). D'Anville's map appeared in an improved version in 1765 (Plate 7-a); not only was it reprinted many times, but it was used by the French Army when it first went to Egypt in 1798. D'Anville gives the name *Tmaié* or *Tmaié* for Thmuis, one often used.

Even after the publication of new maps of Egypt based on Sicard, cartographers continued to copy Paul Lucas' imaginative map (Plate 6-a) indiscriminately, embroidering on it with additions based on hearsay, not on autopsy. A good example of the maps based on inadequate information is one made by Johann B. Homann (1663–1724), entitled *Aegyptus Hodierna*, at a scale of approximately 1:2,300,000 (Plate 7-b). His heirs first published it in a comprehensive atlas in 1731, and in subsequent editions for the next fifty years.

A new folio map of Egypt (Plate 7-c) was published in a *Description of Egypt* (London, 1743) by Richard Pococke (1704–1765). It appears to be based on the *Thronos Alexandrinos* (Plate 5-a) which Pococke had obtained on his visit to Jerusalem in 1722. Evidently unaware of Sicard's work, he places *Timei* too far to the east on the shore of Lake Menzaleh. Although Pococke had been to Egypt, he did not visit Mendes.[38] His mislocation of *Timei* was repeated on Delta maps until well into the nineteenth century.

Didier Robert de Vaugondy (1723–1786) published a *Carte de l'Egypte ancienne et moderne* in 1753. It is based on "R. P. Sicard et autres," at a scale of approximately 1:1,700,000 (Plate 7-d). In 1757 it was incorporated in an *Atlas Universel*. In general it follows Sicard's map but, with reference to our site, Vaugondy prefers Pococke's map of 1743 where, less accurately, *Timei* is located on the shore of Lake Menzaleh.

Among numerous other French cartographers of the eighteenth century, Rigobert Bonne (1727–1794) may serve as an example, whose maps of Egypt from 1762 for the next twenty-five years are based almost entirely on secondary information (Plate 7-e). Unlike Sicard and d'Anville who made by far the best maps of their time and never mention the town of *Mendes*, Bonne at least tries to locate it correctly, just to the north of *Thmuis*. Also, it should be mentioned that Bonne's map of Egypt of 1786 is the first since Mercator's in the sixteenth century to introduce a more accurate projection which was named after him.[39]

A map perhaps based on Bonne, showing Mendes and

Thmuis, forms the frontispiece to volume II of Mr. de P. . . [Corneille de Pauw's *Recherches philosophiques sur les Egyptiens et les Chinois* (Paris, 1773).

In 1798, on a map of the *Entrances to the Nile* (Plate 8-a), "drawn from the latest authorities," W. Heather, of an English map company, again uses Pococke's map as a base. Nevertheless, it includes information derived from Norden, the traveler, Savary,[40] and Sicard. It was occasioned by the Napoleonic invasion which aroused a new interest in Egypt. Following Pococke, *Timei* is located near Lake Menzaleh, but according to Heather's key is now "not visible." *Thmai*, located approximately correctly to the east of Mansurah, is shown by the symbol as a "Small Village," although in this edition of his map Heather does not seem to realize that it is the same place. It appears a third time, near the Mendesian branch of the Nile, northwest of Mansurah, as *Thmus*.

The most significant event in the modern cartography of Egypt occurred in 1798 when, at the beginning of July, the Napoleonic Expedition landed near Alexandria. Bonaparte brought with him, not only a large army, but also a company of artists and scholars, among them nineteen civil engineers and sixteen surveyors and cartographers.[41] They were organized into the Commission des Sciences et des Arts. The Commission gathered and organized the material for the great *Description de l'Egypte*.[42]

At the beginning of the Expedition the French Army used an improved version of d'Anville's *Missir* map, published in 1765 (Plate 7-a). As d'Anville had never been to Egypt, it too was not entirely adequate,[43] and therefore, as soon as the French arrived, the cartographers began to make a new map. First they drew the Nile from Alexandria to Cairo, then they surveyed the town of Alexandria, and eventually the whole of Egypt.

The *Carte de l'Egypte* drawn by a certain Kauffer, "Ing. au Service de la Sublime Porte à Constantinople le 25 8ᵇʳᵉ 1799" (Plate 8-b) purports to incorporate information from the French Army's survey, culled from loyal sheikhs and from deserters, but it is obviously based on one of d'Anville's maps.[44] *Tmaie* is located quite correctly south of *Ashmum Tanan*, a misreading of d'Anville's *Ashmun-Tanah*.

Two maps of *Lower Egypt, Ancient and Modern*, remarkably accurate for the period, were "Published according to Act of Parliament by James Rennell, Nov. 25th 1799."[45] The *Ancient* map he made "according to the ideas of Herodotus" (Plate

37. *Mendes* II, P. 25.
38. *Mendes* II, P. 24.
39. O. Neugebauer, *The Exact Sciences in Antiquity* (Providence, 1957), p. 227.
40. *Mendes* II, Pp. 26–27.
41. J. Christopher Herold, *Bonaparte in Egypt* (New York, 1962), p. 30.
42. The first edition of the *Description de l'Egypte*, in nine text volumes and eleven plate volumes, appeared between 1809 and 1822; the second edition, reprinted many times, in twenty-six text volumes and twelve plate volumes, including an *Atlas*, appeared between 1821 and 1829. References to the *Description* here are to the second edition.
43. *Description* IX (1829), p. 580; ibid. XVII (1824), p. 441.
44. Kamal states that it was published in London in 1799, which, with the French legends, is surprising.
45. J. Rennell, *The Geographical System of Herodotus* II (London, 1830).

8-c) and, following the Antonine Itinerary,[46] he spells Thmuis as *Thumuis*. On the *Modern* map, giving full credit to d'Anville's expert cartography,[47] Rennell improves on it from "the latest observations." On this map Thmuis is spelled *Themase*, perhaps a misreading of Sicard's *Themuis*.

A *Carte particulière et detaillée du Delta* (Plate 8-d) was published in Paris, also in 1799. At a scale of 1:150,000, it is an inset on the *Carte Physique et Politique de l'Egypte* by E. Mentelle and P. G. Chanlaire. It names more places along the Rosetta and Damietta branches of the Nile than heretofore, and it must therefore be the first map made during the French Expedition to use the information Simonel gathered on the branches of the Nile.[48] *Tmaie* is located correctly and, following d'Anville, is spelled *Tmaïé* on the main map.

The mapping of the Delta regions around Mansurah was assigned to nine members of the Commission des Sciences et des Arts.[49] They included Colonel Jacotin who was also in charge of mapping the whole of Egypt,[50] Gratien le Père[51] and one Alibert who had "lived in the province of Mansurah for a long time."[52] Another member of this group was Emmanuel Legentil whose original map is still preserved in the Château de Vincennes. It is entitled *Carte des frontières de l'Egypte du côté de la Syrie . . . levée par le Citoyen Legentil en l'an 9*. It was thus drawn in 1800, but merely mentions *Thnei el hindi* to the south-east of Mansurah (the map is actually drawn in reverse, with south at the top); it is located on a river or canal connecting one illegible town with another. From the drawing it is quite clear that Legentil never came close to the site and located *Thnei el hindi* from hearsay within a network of canals equally misplaced. As the Nile Delta comprised the part of Egypt most coveted by the French, their maps were apt to be elaborate, if not always as accurate as they might have been.[53]

An important cartographical source of *Feuille 35* (Plate 10-a) in the *Description de l'Egypte*, where it appears in modified form, is a sketch map of the *Route de Salhehieh à Mansourah*. It was made on a march of the First Division of the French Army under General Dugua, which took place August 12–16 (or, according to another source, August 13–18), 1798. The original sketch is preserved in the Archives des Cartes, Château

de Vincennes; a portion of it is reproduced here (Plate 8-e). An error, namely that the road passes through *Robey* (El Rub'a), to the south instead of to the east of the *Ruines de Thmuis*, is based on the sketch map. It was first used, however, for the Delta map published in Vivant Denon's *Voyage dans la Basse et la Haute Egypte* I (Paris, 1802). There, of the numerous names that appear on the way to *MANSURA*, only *Mitali* and *Robey* are mentioned.

The information on the sketch map was incorporated in a neatly printed and labeled map preserved in the Château de Vincennes (Plate 8-f). On *Feuille 35* (Plate 9-b), however, the route passes between *Maïéh* and *El Béïdah* and continues correctly to the east of *El Robai*, but the relationship to *RUINES DE THMUIS* is incorrect, because the march also passed to the east of Tell Timai and Tell el Rub'a, and the village of *Roûm* on *Feuille 35* is indeed identical with *El Robai* to the southeast. Thus the cartographers of *Feuille 35* must have tried to reconcile at least two different sources: the route map of the march of the First Division and the survey of Jacotin's detachment, made in the following year. There was no one to explain to them how the various sources of information complemented each other.

By 1809, when the *Description* maps first appeared, the name spelled *Elmâie* on the sketch map of 1799 was changed on *Feuille 35* (Plate 10-a) to *TMÎ EL EMDÎD* (Timai el Amdid) with a large mound next to it indicating the nearby ruins.

Of the four *Description* maps reproduced here (Plate 9-a to -d), Thmuis first appears on the *CARTE HYDROGRA-PHIQUE DE LA BASSE ÉGYPTE. | CARTE DRESSÉE D'APRÈS LES OPÉRATIONS DES ASTRONOMES | ET DES INGÉNIEURS DE L'ARMÉE D'ORIENT | Pour servir au Mémoire sur le Canal des deux Mers*. It is on a scale of 1:400,000 (Plate 9-a).

The savants of the French Expedition knew from Classical authors, as well as from Bonne,[54] of the existence of an ancient site called Mendes and they tried to locate it on their maps. Thmuis was easily enough identified, as the modern name of the nearby village, *Tmî el Emdîd*, reflected it. They supposed that the town of Mendes was in the Mendes Nome and probably near the Mendesian River. Therefore they located it at the nearest major ruins to the north of Thmuis, with the modern name of *Tell el Débéléh* (Tell Etbelleh) and faithfully recorded it as *Mendes ruinée* on the map (Plate 9-a).[55] Jomard, who wrote the chapter on Thmuis for the *Description*,[56] says that a question mark should have been added to the attribu-

---

46. See above P. 4.

47. Rennell, op. cit., p. 200.

48. P. Pallary, "Le corps des ingénieurs géographes de l'Armée d'Orient," in *Géographie* 66 (December, 1936), pp. 285–311. Pallary does not give Simonel's first name, but states that he was a cousin of Colonel Jacotin.

49. *Description* XVII (1824), p. 649.

50. Ibid., p. 448.

51. Ibid., p. 480.

52. *Mendes* II, P. 50. Bertrand Alibert, born on October 28, 1776, at Villeneuve d'Agen (Lot-et-Garonne), was an officer of engineers with Napoleon's Army in Egypt; he died on September 20, 1808. Nothing further concerning his activities in Egypt has come to light in the numerous enquiries kindly undertaken by Mr. J. J. Clère, formerly of the *Ecole Pratique des Hautes Etudes* in Paris.

53. For the trials and tribulations of the surveyors whose chronometer failed them at least once before arriving in Egypt and their attempts to match data derived by diverse means of observation, see Villiers Stuart, "Napoleon's Map of the Nile Delta," in *The Cairo Scientific Journal* 8 (1914), pp. 272–274.

54. See above, P. 7.

55. Mendes was not located correctly until 1871 when H. Brugsch recognized the close proximity of Thmuis and Mendes, and identified the North Kom with the latter (*Mendes* II, P. 93). Thus, whenever Mendes appears on a map before 1871, it does not refer to our site.

Before Brugsch definitely proved that Thmuis and Mendes lay side by side at the same place, William Hamilton, who visited the Delta with Colonel Leake in 1802, had already so surmised (*Mendes* II, P. 51).

56. *Mendes* II, Pp. 39–48.

tion of Mendes, but was omitted.[57] On the map of ancient Egypt in the *Description* (Plate 9-d), Mendes is placed still further to the north, at modern *Achmoun, r.* (Ashmûn er-Rumman) as *Mendes?*

The second map on which Thmuis is shown is a *Carte géographique de l'Egypte*, plate 2 in the front matter of the *Atlas*.

The main body of the *Atlas* consists of forty-two *Feuilles* thus numbered. *Feuille 35*, entitled *MANSOÛRÂH, SÂN*, has by far the most detailed map of the *RUINES DE THMUIS* (Plate 9-b). This constitutes the third map of the *Description de l'Egypte* which shows Thmuis; it gives the most complete account of this part of the Delta thus far.

The fourth Expedition map locating Thmuis is the *Carte des anciennes branches du Nil* (Plate 9-c). As stated along the lower edge it was *Dressée d'après la Carte hydraulique* [sic] *et quelques Reconnaissances par M. Dubois-Aymé* who traveled about the Delta in the autumn of 1799.[58] If this map is based primarily on Dubois-Aymé's trip, then it would predate Colonel Jacotin's official survey of the province which did not begin until June, 1800.[59]

The fifth Delta map in the *Description* is the historical map (Plate 9-d). It is entitled *Carte ancienne et comparée de la Basse Egypte* and is based on the *Carte hydrographique*, the first of the *Description* maps. It was drawn by Colonel Jacotin and Jomard on a scale of 1:500,000.

A map of Lower Egypt on the same scale as the *Carte hydrographique*, locating but not naming the site, is on file in the British Museum.[60] It may be one of the maps never properly published but prepared at Napoleon's request and presented to him on October 16, 1803.[61]

In view of the French preoccupation with Delta cartography, it is not surprising that the great sites of antiquity, such as Sais, Bubastis, and Behbeit el Higara, were drawn with remarkable accuracy. The site marked *Ruines de Thmuis* is unfortunately an exception.

The *Carte hydrographique*, the first of the *Description* maps, bears a tell-tale error, the misdirection of the *Ruines de Thmuis*. The error appears not only in the first edition of 1818 but also on all other *Description* maps of the Delta.

Since, in ancient as well as modern times, the long axis of the site is in a north-south, rather than an east-west direction, the *RUINES DE THMUIS* as shown in great detail on *Feuille 35* (Plate 10-a) must have been turned at a right angle because, when rotated 90° counterclockwise (Plate 10-b), the outline of the ruins corresponds almost exactly to the present-day outline of the North Kom. The Kom is represented by hachures that

terminate at a dotted line indicating a road or footpath. This line clearly marks the break in slope that separates the mound from the surrounding plain. Each major and most of the minor irregularities of the outline conform to the terrain as it is today. Also, on what would now be the northwest section of the mound, there is a small dark rectangle within a larger lighter rectangular area indicated by a stippled pattern. It is labeled *Monolithe* and undoubtedly represents the Great Naos.

According to the scale of *Feuille 35*, the site of the *RUINES DE THMUIS* covers 3,900 meters in length and 1,600 meters in its greatest width, at the latitude of the Naos. The figures were obtained by measuring within the dotted line neatly denoting the extent of the site when the French cartographers were there. Today, however, the distance from the southern end of Tell Timai to the northern end of Tell el Rub'a, the South and North Koms, amounts to only a little over 3000 meters, and the width at the latitude of the Naos now measures a mere 950 meters. It appears therefore that the measurements refer to the ruins of both Koms, but that the survey notes of the South Kom were either lost or ignored, for the *RUINES DE THMUIS* on the *Description* maps in fact include only the North Kom on an exaggerated scale. Assuming, on the other hand, that the ruins on the map were meant to represent the massive remains of both Koms then, when *Feuille 35* is turned, the *Monolithe* is located too far to the south. The Great Naos was perhaps originally meant to be represented by a small square a little further north. The engraver in Paris evidently misinterpreted the drawings on which he based his work, and it would be interesting to trace the original field notes of the French Expedition to understand how the error occurred. The symbol to the "east" of the dark rectangle represents the tomb of *Cheik Emir Abdallah*, but in reality the tomb is located to the southwest of Tell el Rub'a, as though in this case the outline of the Kom had been reversed.

In studying the immediate surroundings of *RUINES DE THMUIS* (Plate 10-a), we are struck by the fact that *El Senbellâoûîn* (es-Simbilâwein) lies southeast instead of southwest of it near *K. El Gorab*. *Zafar* too is misplaced and should be northeast of Thmuis, somewhat southeast of *Tannâh*; we have already discussed the relationship of *Roum* and *El Robaï* (Page 8). Almost all of the other places, however, especially the ancient sites, are located correctly.

In preparing the field maps for publication after their return to France, Napoleon's cartographers referred to a number of additional maps.[62] Among them was L. S. de La Rochette's *Lower Egypt and the Adjacent Deserts* published in London in 1802 (Plate 10-c). It is on a scale of 1:750,000 and shows *Tinahie*, to which as elsewhere on this map the ancient name, in this case *Thmuis*, has been added in a different font and underlined. *Tinahie* is a misspelling which is used again on an English map of Egypt which John Cary published, "from the latest and best

57. *Mendes* II, P. 46, Note 1. Actually, Jomard's reference is to *Feuille 35* of the *Atlas*; see below. It was added in the second edition (Plate 9-b), but omitted on other maps, for instance, the hydrographic map (Plate 9-a).

58. *Description* XV (1826), pp. 169 ff.

59. *Description* XVII (1824), p. 456.

60. British Museum Map Room 64390 (3).

61. *Description* XVII (1824), p. 478.

62. *Description* XVII (1824), pp. 616–617.

authorities," in 1808. The place is in its approximate true geographical position, as is also Tanis to the east.

In 1801 members of the British Expedition to Egypt took the cartographical notes which formed the basis for *A Map / of / Lower Egypt / from / Various Surveys / communicated by / Major Bryce and other Officers / Drawn by A. Arrowsmith, Hydrographer to H.R.H. the Prince of Wales. / 1807.* A copy is preserved by the Ministère de la Guerre in the Château de Vincennes. To the southeast of *Mansoura*, on the road to *Salaheh*, a place named *Maille* appears. Its location corresponds approximately to that of *Maïéh* on earlier maps of the French Expedition. Since no other place names are given on that road until *Labaidi*, further to the east, the author obviously did not visit the site and must have marked it from hearsay. The same *Maille* also occurs on Leake's map (Plate 10-d).

A *Map of Egypt*, "compiled from the most authentic materials and founded on the best Astronomical observations," was made by Lt. Col. W. M. Leake (1777–1860) on a visit to Egypt with William Hamilton[63] in 1801–1802.[64] It is at a scale of 1:700,000 (Plate 10-d). Like Richard Pococke, he places *Tel Etmai* on Lake Menzaleh, directly to the north of Tanis. The map was first published in London in 1818 and, in spite of numerous inaccuracies, was reprinted at intervals until 1882.

An English Egyptologist who made good use of the newly published maps of the *Description* was James Burton (1788–1862).[65] He drew a tracing of the Delta from the hydrographic map of Lower Egypt (Plate 9-a) and apparently took it with him when he visited Mendes in August, 1828. Of interest here is the sketch map which he made in situ (Plate 11-a). It is at a scale of about 1:550,000.

Burton was the first to mark two separate Koms, though with one designation, *TEL TMAI*. He placed a dot east of the South Kom, obviously locating the village of *TMAI*, and to the northeast of the North Kom a dot marked *Roob*. Furthermore, to the southwest of the South Kom another dot denotes *Emeer Abdullah*. For the first time Burton positions all three villages as we know them today.

We find in his diary, August 16–18, 1828,[66] that he went to the site from Mansurah (which he names very lightly in pencil on the sketch map), via *Sandoob*, *Shouwy* (Shawa), *Coom edderbe* (Kom el Derbi) and *Tilbàny*, all easily identifiable. To the southwest of *Tilbàny*, he notes *TEL SEBÀCH*, today Tell Baqlieh, and says "(see)".

On the way from Mansurah via *Tilbàny* Burton may have traveled on the El Masfa Canal, because he draws it correctly for some distance east of *Tilbàny*. Further east he finds *Marsh Lands*, to the north of which he had visited in the beginning of August a *TEL with Granite fragments*, undoubtedly modern Tell Etbelleh [*Tell el Débéléh* or *Mendes*, on the *Description*

maps]. He must also have seen Salamoon and other places along the *Bahr Mansoora*.[67]

Since Burton's sketch map indicates *MEET GHAMR*, it is interesting to note that on his drawing of the North Kom[68] near the Naos, he remarks, "The water comes up here from Meet Ghamr." On his sketch map he also notes that Colonel Leake "improperly placed" *Tel Etmai* to the northeast of *San* (Tanis) on his map of Egypt.[69]

During his travels in Egypt between 1818 and 1827, Pascal Coste (1787–1879), the French architect to Mohammed Ali, made a *Carte de la Basse Egypte*. Although dated 1826, it was published in Paris in 1830 at a scale of 1:600,000 (Plate 11-b). For the region under discussion it constitutes a vast improvement over the Delta maps published in the *Description*. Coste names the Mendes site *Tel Mait*, enclosing it in a circle of dots surrounding a smaller circle of finer dots, and marks it "G. R." (*Grandes Ruines*). His map is remarkable in establishing, for the first time, the correct geographical relation, to the southwest, of *Semboulouvem* and, to the northwest, of *Mansoure*. It shows Lower Egypt divided into eight provinces and sixteen districts.[70]

On his *Carte historique*, also published in 1830, Pierre Lapie claims indebtedness to Coste and to the Napoleonic Commission des Sciences et des Arts, with other cartographers.[71] Lapie uses a designation similar to that of Coste for the site, namely *Tell Mait*, which reappears on maps of Egypt until as late as 1882. His map is at a scale of 1:1,200,000.

In 1831 in London, the Society for the Diffusion of Useful Knowledge printed two maps, *Ancient Egypt* (Plate 11-c) and (modern) *Egypt*, by George Long (1800–1879), at about 1:1,000,000. On the map of *Ancient Egypt*, based apparently on Major Rennell's map (Plate 8-c), Mendes, mislocated, and Thmuis appear. The sites are indicated by a point symbol, a small circle. On the second map Thmuis, as on d'Anville's maps, is called *Tmaié*. While the maps are good examples of cartography, they add nothing new to our knowledge of Egypt or the site. For the *Library of Entertaining Knowledge*, George Long also wrote a catalogue of Egyptian antiquities in the British Museum, in which he theorizes about the Great Naos.[72]

For a long time after the *Description* appeared, few new at-

---

63. W. Hamilton, *Aegyptiaca* (London, 1809), p. 361.

64. *Mendes* II, P. 51.

65. W. R. Dawson and E. P. Uphill, *Who Was Who in Egyptology* (London, 1972), pp. 48–49.

66. *Mendes* II, Pp. 74–81.

67. Actually spelled *Bahr Mansooka* by whoever inked in the names Burton wrote on his map. The town of *Mansoora*, for instance, is spelled correctly but written so faintly that the inscriber missed it. *Marsh Land* and *Lake Menzaleh*, however, are inked in Burton's own hand.

68. *Mendes* II, P. 77.

69. For Colonel Leake's map, see Plate 10-d.

70. This division does not follow that established by the famous 1816 cadastre of Mohammed Ali, by which Lower Egypt was divided into six provinces and 92 districts; see Omar Toussoun, in *Mém. Soc. R. Géog. d'Egypte* VIII,3 (1936). The villages of *El Roubh* and *Toumay el Amdid* are listed on page 452 in the *Khot Tilbana*. Today the *Khot* division of the Delta having been abandoned long since, our site is situated in the *Markaz el-Simbillâwin*; op. cit., VIII,2 (1928), p. 371. For *Khot*, better described as *Ḥod*, see Mostafa el-Amir, "A Statue of Ramesses II," in *ASAE* 42 (1942), p. 359, note 1.

71. H. Lorin, *Bibliographie géographique de l'Egypte* I (Cairo, 1928), p. 70.

72. *Mendes* II, P. 83.

tempts to map Egypt were made. An exception is the *Carte hydrographique de la Basse Egypte* by Linant de Bellefonds (1779–1883). The original is kept in the Archives des Cartes, Ministère de la Guerre, Château de Vincennes, Paris. It is entitled *Carte/ de la/Basse Egypte/et d'une partie de l'isthme de suès/où sont désignés les travaux faits et à faire pour la canalisation/Par/A. Linant./Directeur des Ponts et Chaussées en Egypte et Ingénieur en Chef des Barrages du Nil/D'après ses travaux et ses Observations depuis l'année 1820 jusqu'a l'année 1841.*[73] It is on a scale of 1:250,000 (Plate 11-d). This was obviously Linant de Bellefonds' working copy because some erasures are found directly below Mendes, and it must have served as a basis for the *Carte hydrographique* which, according to Fontaine,[74] was first published in Paris in 1854 and republished by the Ministère de la Guerre in 1855 (Plate 11-e).[75] A corrected edition was published in 1882. Linant shows *Tel Temey el Amdid* in the correct north-south alignment, with two distinct *koms* indicated by a stippled pattern enclosed by a dotted line. Like the manuscript map it is on a scale of 1:250,000 and in general still follows the French *Description* maps of the Delta.[76] Some of the towns, like *Simbillawine*, south of our site, are still almost exactly where Bonaparte's cartographers misplaced them.[77] This map served as the basis for many others in the next decades. Linant de Bellefonds established the location of the two Koms as well as, to the east of *Tel Temey*, the now unidentified *Douuie*.

Lepsius, in his monumental study of Egypt, includes a map of the Nile Delta, dated 1859, by H. Kiepert, which is based on the French Expedition maps, as well as on Linant de Bellefonds' hydrographic map, with all their errors.[78]

Heinrich Brugsch, the first to establish the identity of Mendes with Tell el Rubʿa, designed a *Karte von Unter-Aegypten* entitled *Aegyptus Antiqua* (Plate 12-a) with the names of the twenty Delta nomes superimposed.[79]

By 1878, British economic and political interests in Egypt had greatly increased and with them arose a need for more accurate and detailed maps. In June, 1882, "from an original French Survey in 1818 by M. Jacotin, from the manuscript of Mahmud Bey and from the most recent information," the Intelligence Branch of the British War Office compiled a revised *Map of Lower Egypt* in 4 sheets (Plate 12-b), on a scale

of 1:200,000. Because it shows the two Koms, some of "the most recent information" must have come from Linant's map of 1855. The South Kom is labeled *Ru. of THMUÏS*. The villages of *Er-Rûb* and *Tmey el-Amdîd* appear on the northeast edges of each Kom, with *Kafr-Abdallah* at the southwest edge of the South Kom, all vast improvements on Linant's map, which show that between 1855 and 1882 a new survey must have been made.[80]

It should also be noted that this is the first map to show a place to the south of *Kafr Abdallah* called *Kafr Mohammed-et-Timsah*. "Timsah" is Arabic for "crocodile." It may or may not refer to a local crocodile cult reflected in the typically Mendesian offering tables with crocodile ornamentation (*Mendes* II, Plates 32–35).

Another *Map of Lower Egypt*, dated August 1882, was compiled by the Office of the Chief of Engineers of the United States Army, at a scale of 1:1,000,000. Although it does not show much detail, it is illustrated here (Plate 12-c), because it splits our site among three places, as on Heather's map (Plate 8-a), with variations of Thmuis for their names. Here they are *Thmais*, *Timay el enid*, and *Tel Mait*, scattered about the landscape east of *Mansoura* and north of *Sembouluven*. Like all American maps of Egypt, with the possible exception of the *Tell Râk* sheet (Plate 16-d), it was based on secondary information.

In 1885, Rand McNally, the well-known geographical company in Chicago, published a new map of *The Lower Nile*. While the *Ruins of Thmuis* appear in their approximate true position, the *Ruins of Mendes* are still misplaced to the north,[81] fifteen years after their correct location was discovered.[82]

By 1888 better financial control of Egypt became desirable and a more accurate survey of the taxable land was necessary. Therefore Mahmud Pasha el Falaki, more often referred to as Mahmud Bey,[83] drew up a new map of the Delta in color, at a scale of 1:200,000, with Arabic legends (Plate 12-d). The villages of El Rubʿa, Timai el Amdid and Kafr el Amir Abdallah are correctly located, and a faint contour seems to outline the two Koms. A dot on the western part of the North Kom may be meant to mark the Great Naos. To the northwest of *Kafr el Amir*, approximately halfway between *Timai el Amdid* and *El Tamid el Hagar*, appear *Fasuk* and *Kafr Fasuk*, called El Kamal today. *Simbillawein* is shown correctly in relation to the site.

Also in 1888 a *Carte de la Basse Egypte* appeared in Cairo, on

73. Linant de Bellefonds, *Mémoire sur les principaux travaux d'utilité publique executés en Egypte* (Paris, 1872–73), p. 490.

74. A. Fontaine, *Monographe cartographique de l'Isthme de Suez* II (Cairo, 1955), p. 104.

75. However, a copy kept by the Ministère de la Guerre at the Château de Vincennes is dated "1847" in a fine, obviously contemporary hand.

76. J. Mazuel, *L'oeuvre géographique de Linant de Bellefonds* (Cairo, 1937), pp. 8, 115.

77. For example, on the polychrome *Carte de la Basse Egypte et Du Canal Maritime de Suez* by Desbuissons (Paris, 1880), at a scale of 1:500,000 (Harvard College Library 2390/13). *Simbillawine* is, however, distinctly to the southeast of our site, thus employing on the one hand Linant de Bellefonds' improvement, but on the other hand repeating some of the mistakes of the *Description*.

78. C. R. Lepsius, *Denkmaeler* I (Berlin, 1859), plate 3.

79. The map was first published by J. C. Hinrichs for H. Brugsch, *L'exode et les monuments égyptiens* (Leipzig, 1875) and by John Murray as an appendix to Brugsch's *A History of Egypt* (London, 1879) and where, strangely enough, the date of the map is given as 1877.

80. The new survey may also be reflected in a map which we have not seen but which is listed in Lorin, *Bibl. géogr.* I (1928), p. 73, no. 1047: *Basse-Egypte (Carte de la) dressée . . . pour le service de 'administration des domaines affectés en garantie de l'emprunt contracté le 31 octobre 1878. Echelle, 1:400,000—Paris, 1882.*

81. It is interesting to note in this connection that the Delta map which A. Gayet includes in his *Itinéraire illustré de la Haute Egypte* (Paris, [1893]), the *Ruines de Mandès* [sic] are still misplaced way to the north of *Tel-el-Thmeï*.

82. *Mendes* II, p. 93.

83. Mahmoud el Falaki is indeed the same as the Mahmud Bey of the 1855 map at a scale of 1:400,000, as shown by nos. 1041 and 1238 in Lorin, op. cit., pp. 73, 87, as well as by Omar Toussoun, *Géographie de l'Egypte à l'époque arabe*.

a scale of 1:400,000, with *THMUIS* referring to both Koms. *Fassouka* and *K.* (Kafr) *Fassouka* on this map (Plate 12-e) indicate the influence of Mahmud el Falaki's map with the Arabic legends, although more topographical detail is given here than on his map. Both Koms are located in their true geographical position by fine hachuring and, for the first time, a line running from southwest to northeast appears between them; a legend further to the southwest identifies it as *C. el Shon*, the modern El Shiwan Canal (see Plate 16-d). A pencil line which originates at the *S* in *Simbellawein*, running north, through our site and to the northwest, may constitute an attempt to locate the Mendesian branch of the Nile.[84] The legend *MENDES*, faintly penciled in above *THMUIS*, appears on the copy in the Collège de France, which is illustrated here (Plate 12-e).

This is perhaps the place to introduce an unpublished map also in the Collège de France. It is taken from the hand-drawn and hand-colored *Atlas Archéologique de l'Egypte* by Georges Daressy (1864–1938), at a scale of 1:250,000.[85] It is undated, and he may well have made it early in this century if not at the end of the last. The page showing *Tell el Rob'a* and *Tmai el Emdid* is illustrated now (Plate 13-a), however, because in 1890 Daressy wrote an important description of the place.[86] The South Kom appears much larger than the North Kom, although today they are nearly equal in size. Daressy numbered the South Kom "S.109" and the North Kom "S.110." These figures refer to the *Liste des tells et koms à sebakh* (Cairo, 1915), where, on page 11, Mendes is listed as *Temaï el Amdid* and *el Rabaa*.[87] In sketching the Koms, Daressy liberally applied the principle of cartographic generalization; none of the nearby villages is indicated. He drew in the long linear ridge of *Tell el Qenan* extending to the east;[88] even the great sand ridge near *Sangaha*, southeast of Mendes, is shown in its correct location and approximate true shape. It is clear from this map that Daressy had an excellent knowledge of the archaeological sites of the Delta, a fact known from his numerous publications on Lower Egypt.[89]

In 1896, the Public Works Ministry, through the Inspector General of Irrigation in Lower Egypt, produced an excellent Arabic map in color of *Daqahliya Province* (Plate 13-b) at a scale of 1:100,000.[90] The two Koms are separated by the *El Shun* canal and they are represented by finely drawn hachures

arranged in concentric bands to indicate increasing elevation toward the center. The North Kom is labeled *Tell el Rub'a* and the South Kom *Tell Timai*. This is the first published map on which both Koms are identified by their modern names. The outlines of the Koms and the alignment of the long axes are very close to the way they appear today.

In the same year, 1896, the Public Works Ministry published another map of *Daqahliya Province* (Plate 13-c) at 1:100,000, with English legends. Although it gives *Tall er Rob'* and *Tall Timayy* it can hardly be the English version of the preceding map, because neither of the two Koms is shown and there are other differences. Still, the villages and *'Ez.* (farms) may have been copied from the same survey on which the Arabic map is based.

In 1897, Audébeau, Sauter and Colani published in Cairo a *Carte de la Basse Egypte* (Plate 13-d) at a scale of 1:200,000. By means of double circles of light hachures it shows two distinct Koms. Their outlines do not conform, however, to those of the present day, but the *C. el Chon* separates them, as on maps from now on. From *Ghorour* east of the North Kom, angling across the northern part of the South Kom, a road connects *Tmay el Amdid* with *Kafr Amir Abdallah* and farther to the west with *Miniet Gharitah*. The road corresponds approximately to the modern road. Although the name *Thmuis* appears in large print close to the South Kom, it may refer to both Koms.

The *Nouvelle Carte Générale* by E. Nicohosoff was published in Alexandria some time after 1900. A simplified map, evidently prepared for tourists, it merely locates the village of *Tami el-Amdid*.

In 1902–1903 the Survey Department in Cairo issued a new set of maps, 1:50,000. A section of Sheet 55 of the revised edition, published in color in 1908, is reproduced on Plate 14-a. It gives place names in both Arabic and English, and is the first modern map to show vegetation, swamps and clumps of trees. The two Koms are indicated by groups of broken curved lines, in plan view looking like flowers. Except for the railroad, which in maps after 1916 cuts across the north end of the South Kom, all essential features, such as roads, canals and villages, are in their proper location as we know them today and show that there has been little change in the area since the turn of the century.

The North Kom is labeled *Tel el Qasr* ("Castle Hill") which in 1958 is still found on the United States Army map of the region (Plate 16-d). Its use appears strange since, on maps as early as 1896 (Plate 13-b), the site was labeled *Tell el Rub'a*. The South Kom is unlabeled; only the names of the two adjoining villages are given. The Koms are separated by the

84. Bietak, *Tell el-Dab'a* II (Vienna, 1975) pp. 94, 232.

85. Jean Yoyotte was the first to draw our attention to it; its reproduction was kindly permitted by Professor G. Posener of the Collège de France.

86. *Mendes* II, Pp. 104–111.

87. This *Liste* is identified on the title page as an "Extrait du *Journal officiel* du Gouvernement égyptien du Samedi 12 février 1910." It is known to us only from a copy in the Library of the Egyptian Museum in Cairo. The sites are not numbered, but beginning with Tell Basta on page 8 as "S. 1," "S. 109" and "S. 110" are indeed the numbers which, on his map, Daressy gave our site. It may well be that Daressy annotated his own copy with these numbers and transferred them to his hand-drawn map.

88. Pl. 27-e and P. 22.

89. *Mendes* II, Pp. 104 ff.

90. According to a publication of the Ministry of Finance, Survey Department, entitled *A List of Maps, Plans and Publications Published up to 31st December 1907* (Cairo, 1908), p. 19, maps for Daqahalia Province on the scales of 1:2,500, 1:50,000

and 1:100,000 were available at that time or had been planned. It then reads, "Province Maps. Daqahalia Province map, scale 1:100,000, published in 1896 in 4 sheets, price 120 mills. per sheet, English or Arabic edition." On page 5, par. 2, it says that "Copies of the original field sheets of Sharqia, Daqahlia and Beheira Provinces, of the survey of 1892–1898, scale 1/10,000, can be obtained." Page 12 of the same publication indicates that cadastral maps of all villages are printed in Arabic only and are available for Daqahaliya on a scale of 1:2,500.

Shuan Canal. The north end of *Tel el Qasr* is crossed by the agricultural road which still exists and which leads to the head-quarters of the expedition, Mendes House.[91] Near the village of *El Roba'* this road connects with a road running southwest to *Kafr el Amir Abdalla*, along the course of the *Shuan Canal*. The copy in the Collège de France reproduced here (Plate 14-a) is annotated in Daressy's hand.

A portion of what is probably the first Postal Map of the Delta is included (Plate 14-b), because it shows that the main line of communications near our site came from *Sinbillawen*, past *Kr. el Amir*. Neither of the Koms is indicated. The village of El Rub'a does not appear. The map is dated 1906.

In 1912 the Survey Department of Egypt published a new Delta map in one sheet at a scale of 1:200,000 (Plate 14-c) which, at approximately the same time, was also put out as a *Mean Tax Rate* map. While the latter, according to its purpose, merely indicates the villages, the former by a kind of dotted shading shows both the North and South Koms. The distance between the Koms is greater on the map than in reality, but the villages and major roads are in their proper orientation. An Arabic version appeared in 1914 at a reduced scale of 1:250,000 (Plate 14-e).

In 1913 the Survey of Egypt again published a series of Delta maps on a scale of 1:50,000 (Plate 14-d) which, for the Mendes region, shows a number of small improvements although, unlike the 1908 revised map (Plate 14-a), it does not give contour lines for the two Koms. The map is in color; names are printed in Arabic and English. The letter "P" indicates a post office, "T" a telegraph office, and the letter "R" a regulator or sluice.

Both Koms are shown on this excellent map by carefully placed dots in shaded relief. The outlines of the Koms conform closely to their present shape. Darker shading evidently indicates steeper slopes. The Koms are correctly labeled as TEL EL RUB' and TEL TEMAI EL AMDÎD, and the *Shuwan Canal* passes between them. Features of the terrain also conform to those on present-day maps of the site. Located on the northern part of the North Kom is a triangular point symbol. On United States topographic maps it would represent a bench mark or triangulation point. It may have been a fixed point for a survey half a century ago and appears as a numbered bench mark on maps as recently as 1941 (Plate 15-e). A rectangular enclosure on the west side of the North Kom may represent both the area of the Great Naos and the Ram Cemetery, incorrectly placed.

The 1913 map must have been the basis for a new map in color at a scale of 1:100,000. Put out in a provisional issue in 1915, it was published in 1916 and issued again in a revised edition in 1917 (Plate 15-a). The Koms are indicated by a stippled dot pattern, surrounded by four, five and six meter contour lines in almost concentric circles. This is the first map with the spur of the narrow gauge railway running from Man-

surah via Timai el Amdid to Sadakah and beyond, still in use today. As on the 1913 map, a triangular symbol denotes the bench mark just south of the agricultural road crossing the north end of the North Kom.

The standard map series of 1:100,000 was brought up to date by a new edition in 1926 (Plate 15-b). As a further improvement over the 1917 edition, it marks the eight, ten and twelve meter contour lines. On *Tell el Rub'* a "14" meter indication locates the bench mark of that elevation above sea level on the Kom.

In 1929 the Survey Department produced a *Communications Map of Lower Egypt* at a scale of 1:300,000. It does not indicate the two Koms, only the villages of *El Roba*, *Temai el Amdid*, and *Kr. el Amir Abdalla*.

On the basis of the 1:100,000 map of 1926 a new Delta map at a scale of 1:250,000 was published by the British War Office in 1933. It appeared in a second edition in 1941; Plate 15-c illustrates the region of Mendes from Sheet 2, entitled *Port Said*, of this wartime Delta map.

In 1930–1935 the Survey Department brought out a new map series of 1:25,000 in color. The Mendes area is found on sheet $\frac{91}{660}$ entitled *Umm el Diyâb*, dated 1934 (Plate 15-d). This large scale map in Arabic shows the two Koms with the five meter contour lines. Within the contours a shaded pattern has been placed over the Koms which are drawn in such detail that they include footpaths and the outlines of some of the enclosure walls. Since the map was made, hardly any changes have occurred in major cultural features associated with the site. In addition to the main captions, both Koms include names in smaller print, which apparently the local population has given to individual parts of each Kom. For instance, the Great Naos is referred to as *Qaṣr Bint el Yahûdy* ("Castle of the Jew's Daughter"). The frequent occurrence of the term *Goset* may go back to the ram worship of ancient times. Near the center of the North Kom, below the bench mark 13.6 meters, appear two names: *Wady el Malakhat* and *Birket es-Suk*. They refer appropriately to the rectangular and at times salt-covered depression thought to have once been the Sacred Lake. Because of its nearly level surface, it may be likened to a market place (*suk*).[92]

This map served as the basis for the 1941 *Ägypten* map at the same scale. It was produced by the General Staff of the German Army (Plate 15-e) which, significantly enough, mentions the *Qaṣr Bint el-Yahûdi* on the North Kom, although it leaves off all other local names of the site. The designation *antikes Grab* is way out of place and should be further west, so as to refer to the Dynasty VI tomb chapel discovered on the North Kom in July, 1907,[93] or perhaps the so-called sarcophagus of King Nepherites (Plate 32) is meant.

A map of Egypt made in 1938 at a scale of 1:1,000,000 is based on Survey of Egypt sheets dated 1933–1937 at a scale of

---

91. For Mendes House, first built in April, 1964, and extensively remodeled since then, see Plate 28 and the map on Plates 17–19.

92. See below, P. 22.
93. Plate 31-a; *Mendes* II, P. 191, **6**.

1:500,000. The *MENDES THMUIS* site appears in two triangles of dots with the railroad passing between them (Plate 16-a).

The Egyptian Railways Map of June, 1939, on a scale of 1:400,000 merely gives the railroad stations of the Mendes area. The *Communications Map of Lower Egypt*, 1:300,000, 1950 edition, follows the 1929 edition in outline (see above). The names of the three villages read *El Rub'*, *Timai el Amdîd*, and *Kr. el Amir Aballa* (sic); the site is blotted out by the second letter of *DAQAHALIYA*.

In 1951 the Survey Department published a series of maps at a scale of 1:100,000 consisting of individual sheets in color with Arabic legends. On Sheet $\frac{30,30}{31,00}$ entitled *Sharq Tanta* (Plate 16-b) both Koms are shown by contour lines; only the North Kom is labeled. In 1952 a second edition of Sheet $\frac{91}{660}$ of the 1:25,000 series was published, this time named *Tâg el 'Izz* (Plate 16-c). Cartographically the changes are minor, but the new map takes cognizance of the advance made upon the Koms by the surrounding fields. For instance, on the west side of the north part of the North Kom, the 1934 map (Plate 15-d) shows a dotted area which is plain white in the 1952 map, thus indicating that this terrain had been placed under cultivation, as it is today. Also, the 1952 edition relocated some of the Arabic captions, as for instance one west of the great East Wall on the North Kom. This map has English names superimposed for villages, farms and other features. A curious mistake occurs on the North Kom where, directly below *Tell el-Rub'* appears (*Tell el-Qaṣṣ*) instead of *Tell el Qaṣr*.[94]

In 1958 the U.S. Army Map Service, Corps of Engineers, printed a series of topographic maps of the Nile Delta in color at a scale of 1:50,000. Sheet 5686 of Series P 773, entitled *Tell Râk*, includes the Mendes area (Plate 16-d). The two Koms are distinctly outlined by a five-meter contour line with brown shading for further emphasis. The North Kom is labeled with the additional name *Tell el-Qasr* in parenthesis, following the map of 1902–1903 as revised in 1908 (Plate 14-a). Several footpaths cross the Tells. The highest point indicated above sea level on the North Kom is 13.6 meters or about forty-four feet, and on the South Kom 10.4 meters or about thirty-four feet.

The north end of the North Kom is cut by an unpaved road, the agricultural road referred to previously. Angling southeastward, the road intersects another road just south of *El-Rub'*. This second road winds to the southwest between the two Koms, following the course of the *El-Shiwân Can*. Then road and canal pass the north edge of *Kr. el-Amir 'Abdalla* on the northwestern corner of the South Kom. A road, hardly more than a dirt trail, leaves the east edge of the village and

angles eastward across the north end of the South Kom. It follows the narrow gauge railroad between the Koms and passes through the village of *Timai el-Amdîd*. A strange mistake occurs in the English legend below *Tell Timai* where *Gûret el-Waraq* is printed instead of *Goset el-waraq*. Underneath, *El-Riḥâba* refers to the vastness of the Tell behind the village. Except for the Russian map (Plate 16-e), this is the most recent map available and, although it gives less detail than the Survey of Egypt map published in 1952, it has proved extremely accurate in the field.

The last map to be published before the hostilities of June, 1967, is a Russian map of the Delta at a scale of 1:1,000,000, which dates from 1965 (Plate 16-e). Because of its scale no terrain features are shown; only lines of communication, such as waterways and railroads, and place names appear. Among the latter is the local railroad stop of *Тимаи-элб-Амдид* (Timai el Amdid) in its correct geographical location.

Excellent cadastral maps of the Delta are on file in the capital of each province which, for the Mendes region, is Mansurah. The maps are in black and white and, of course, in Arabic, at a scale of about 1:2,500. These maps give details for property definition and farm purposes only. Because the two Koms are Government property and cannot be cultivated, they are not crisscrossed by canals or drains and are not divided into fields. On the map, therefore, they appear as large empty areas. Outlining the Koms almost exactly, the five-meter contour line forms the border between the small field patterns of the agricultural land and the larger subdivisions of the Tells.

In 1965 and 1966 David Stieglitz, then architect of the Mendes Expedition, prepared a Master Survey Plan of Tell el Rub'a and Tell Timai in black and white at a scale of 1:3,000 which is discussed in Chapter II. It shows the site topographically by the use of fifty centimeter contour lines and indicates the position of ancient stone blocks, including the rams' coffins, observed at the beginning of the excavations in May, 1964 (Plate 17).

In conclusion, it becomes evident that the history of the cartography of the Mendes-Thmuis region is generally that of the whole Delta. It can be divided into four partly overlapping main periods.

The first period begins in the middle of the second century A.D. with Ptolemy the Geographer whose map was copied and adapted for well over a thousand years.

The second phase is that of the eighteenth century travelers who drew new maps based mainly on their own observations.

The third period results from a joint effort of the French Army cartographers, from 1798 to the date of publication, in the first scientific mapping of the Delta.

The fourth and latest period began with the British Army maps of 1882, which introduced the cartographic work of the new Survey of Egypt.

---

94. Another error in the captions is evident from *Timai el-Amdid & Kafr Muḥammad el-Timsâḥ* which appears on Plate 16-c. Kafr Muhammed el Timsâh no longer exists. From 1882 through 1941 (Plates 12-b to 15-c) it appears to the southwest of Tell Timai, on the Buhiya Canal.

II

A NEW MAP OF MENDES

By DAVID STIEGLITZ

Before the Mendes Expedition began its excavations in 1964, no topographic survey of either Tell el Rub'a or Tell Timai appears to have been made. The only evidence for a general cadastral survey is a series of steel rail markers left standing in the Delta from the Survey of Egypt's work there in 1933–1934.[1] Here we shall describe the topographic surveying and general mapping techniques employed at Mendes during the three excavation seasons from 1964–1966 (Plates 17–26).[2]

In selecting a basic method for surveying the topography of the two Koms, we had to consider the great area involved, the limited amount of time at our disposal, and the fact that essentially only the architect would execute the survey. In principal, the "Controlling-point Method" was used; however, this method was adopted with the stipulations that a theodolite be substituted for the plane table alidade and that the formula used in stadia reduction computations be simplified.[3]

Having established a system for data gathering, it was necessary to obtain a fixed level above sea level, a taped base line, and an azimuth off of True North. This information was required in order to avoid a relative system of heights, to have a basis for all triangulation and polygon figures, and to establish a North-South grid.

A fixed position above sea level was obtained through the help of two bench marks in the vicinity, near the mounds of Tell el Rub'a and Tell Timai.[4] Normal differential leveling processes made it possible to establish an ASL (Above Sea Level) reading for points on the North and South Koms which came close to these bench marks.[5]

The base line was defined as part of a line already established in the excavation area of 1964 by the acting architect, G. R. H. Wright. This line presumably lay on the main north-south axis of the Temple and had been used with a perpendicular line to establish a coordinate grid for excavation purposes.[6] Two coordinate points on that north-south line were chosen as the limits of the base line for the survey.[7]

A true azimuth for the north-south Temple Grid Axis was established by using the aforementioned line between points "A" and "B," and observing Polaris from a third point.[8]

With this basic information at hand, i.e. a fixed elevation above sea level, a taped base line, and an azimuth off True North, it was possible to proceed with the topographic survey. Since, on the North Kom, the Precinct Wall provided the most suitable view of the surrounding tell, the first polygon

---

1. The locations of these rails were later incorporated into our topographic system as polygon points. They include "O", "M", "A₄", "B", "B₄", and "B₉" on the North Kom, and "V₅", "V₇", "V₈", "B₅", "B₆", and "B₇" on the South Kom.

2. The new maps of the North and South Koms were first published by Hansen, in *JARCE* 4 (1965), pl. XVI, and Ochsenschlager, in *JARCE* 6 (1967), pls. XIX-XX.

3. The two basic expressions for distance (vertical and horizontal) were simplified in the following manner:

Where: K = stadia interval factor f/1
   s = stadia interval
   C = stadia constant f + c
   a = vertical angle of the line of site
(Horizontal distance)
   $H = Ks \cos^2 a + C\cos a$
(Vertical distance)
   $V = \frac{1}{2} Ks \sin 2a + C\sin a$

The K value for all instruments involved in taking stadia data was known to be 100. In most instances C was assumed to be one meter and .01 was then added to the recorded stadia interval, thus negating the second terms of the reduction formulae. Then, acting on the assumption that $\cos^2 a = \cos a$ and $\frac{1}{2}\sin 2a = \sin a$, the standard reduction table could be used and additional compensation factors for C could be eliminated from the computational process.

4. That closest to Tell el Rub'a lies approximately five kilometers south and about four meters east of a large canal bridge; it is officially listed as No. 6560 and has an ASL of 4.245 meters. The second bench mark is located in the west side of a bridge foundation on the main road through Timai, approximately thirteen kilometers east of town; it is listed as No. 6502 and has an ASL of 4.681 meters.

5. An ASL of 6.836 meters was established for point "A₄" on the North Kom, and 4.890 for point "B₅" on the South Kom. Both "A₄" and "B₅" had been established in the British cadastral survey (Plate 15-c).

6. North-South grid lines used Y coordinates, and East-West lines used X coordinates.

7. The points chosen were X 290, Y 130, and X 180, Y 130. They were originally set in well-founded concrete pylons at approximately 110 meters from each other. A series of ten successive tapings later set this interval more accurately at 109.9103 meters. These points became "A" and "B" on the True North Grid.

8. Polaris was observed from a station point over "B₁" on July 5, 1964, at 10:00 P.M. Subsequent calculation and observation provided an azimuth for line "B₁"; "A" of 236 degrees 31 minutes 15 seconds. The north-south Temple Grid Axis (actually Y axis) was then fixed at a true azimuth of 21 degrees 19 minutes 7 seconds.

was set along its ridge. A broad triangulation pattern was established around the areas under excavation, establishing points "B₁", "A", "B", "X", "Y", and "Z". These points were given metric coordinates relative to point "X" which had been chosen as the 0,0 point of the True North Grid. All subsequent polygons were constructed, measured, computed, and adjusted as stadia traverses.[9] Latitude and departures of all sides of all polygons were computed logarithmically.[10]

In the process of surveying the polygon on the Precinct Wall a series of base points, which had been previously staked out, were also recorded. In many cases, it was impossible to describe the Wall base accurately and in other cases no indication was visible at all. In the final rendering the areas which we were sure represented the Wall base were shaded with long strokes, and the conjectural portion of the Wall was bounded by a heavy line and shaded with stippling.

On the North Kom six polygons were set in 1964 in addition to the basic Precinct Wall polygon. Although the lengths of the polygon sides vary considerably, an attempt was made to keep them well under two hundred meters. In all, about 100 points were set and fixed in a definite coordinate relationship to "X" (0,0). For each of the coordinated polygon points approximately 75 to 100 elevation points were then taken within the immediate area depending, of course, on the moulding of the surrounding land forms.[11] Because the terrain on the North Kom varies considerably (see below, Page 20) and the first survey was plotted without the aid of field checking, it became apparent that certain areas would need considerably more detailing. Therefore, two additional polygons were set in 1965 and 20 more points added to the list of master grid coordinates. An approximate total of 500 more elevation points was taken in the area just north of Tell el ʿIzam (N 100–300, E 250–380) and within the area of the "Sacred Lake" (S 200–50, W 15—E 150).

Simultaneous with the elevation data gathering process, certain other non-topographic features were noted by the stadia method and now appear on the maps. The position of large inscribed blocks as they existed on the North Kom at the opening of the 1964 excavation season were noted and are now designated by small black dots within small circles. Their

numerical designation, 1 M I-, is keyed to De Meulenaere's *List of Objects* in *Mendes* II.[12] Basically, they fall into three groupings: N 300–400, E 100–200; N 550–560, W 00–10; N 20–120, W 30–110. The position of numerous ram sarcophagi in situ was noted by the same method, and they also appear as small black dots on the maps. On the North Kom their distribution splits almost exactly into a North and South Cemetery, with a few scattered between; N 260–295, W 120–150 and N 12–25, W 266–295. On the South Kom two fragmentary sarcophagi were noted at the time our survey was run in 1965. These now appear at approximately S 1630–1640; W 15–30. It should be noted here that no attempt was made to depict either size or shape of the blocks, but only to record their basic relationships and positions on the Koms. The only other archaeological features recorded on these maps are the positions of the Naos (Plate 1) on the North Kom and a large limestone platform on the South Kom (Plate 38-c, -d). The location of the Naos (N 00–05; W 32–137) was initially accomplished by triangulation from points "X" and "Z" to an inscribed mark on its sill. The limestone platform was recorded by the stadia method and lies on a relatively flat area of the South Kom (S 1650–1660; E 5–20).

When excavations began on the South Kom during the 1965 season it became quite clear that an extension of the same True North grid system would be very advantageous. This meant that all coordinated points would bear a direct relationship to point "X" on the North Kom. With such an objective, a very long polygon was laid out connecting line $W_u;V$ at the tip of the North Kom with several steel points on the South Kom. The polygon was designated as "V" but does not appear on either map. After the polygon was balanced and relative coordinates affixed to point "V_8" at the northern tip of Tell Timai, five additional polygons were set around the South Kom and subsequently elevation data was taken in exactly the same fashion as on the North Kom.

A cursory inspection of the terrain prior to surveying showed that the central area of the Kom would be impossible to map by conventional methods and that the best we could hope to accomplish would be to define vaguely the periphery of the immense stretch of gutted architectural remains which is shown as a gray form on the plotted topographic map. Since the general land forms surrounding this area were much less contorted than those on the North Kom, very little correction was needed before final rendering could be accomplished; thus no additional polygons were constructed in 1966. A total of about 40 points were fixed in a definite coordinate relationship to "X" and a reference axis of 00, 00—S 2000 was established. For each polygon point set, approximately 75 elevation points were taken with the same distribution pattern as that described for the North Kom.

In 1966 it was decided to locate the areas excavated on the

9. For each side of the polygon two stadia readings were recorded, a foresite from one end and a backsite from the other, then averaged without regard to adjustment. Similarly, a vertical angle was measured from each end of a side and then averaged. Interior horizontal angles were measured and azimuths then computed.

10. In balancing each polygon the "Compass Rule" was employed, primarily because it is easy to apply in long traverses. The rule is that, since it is practically impossible to close a traverse in the field, the correction to the components of any side (in terms of latitude or departure) should be in the same proportion to the length of the entire traverse. This method provides opportunities to check the accuracy of computational work since, after the total traverse is adjusted, it should not only plot as closed, but the balanced latitudes and departures should both total an algebraic zero. In a similar fashion, the elevation of each polygon point could be balanced by treating the data as a vertical traverse; however, in most cases no elevational adjustment proved necessary.

11. In shooting an elevation point we tried not to exceed a linear distance of 75 meters from the instrument station and a full intercept was read and subsequently halved.

12. *Mendes* II, Pp. 191–192, **1–16**.

South Kom during the 1965 and 1966 seasons. Accordingly, points "A", "B", "C", "D", and "E" were set in close proximity to these areas and a triangulation was undertaken from line D_2; D_4. Points "C" and "E" lie immediately adjacent to the 1965 excavations, and points "A" and "B" are located on the extremities of the 1966 trench.

In plotting both maps, the borders of the Koms are indicated by a black line, broken at those places where an actual edge point was sighted. The contours are dashed lines, indexed at the ten-meter interval (the heaviest contour). Enough elevational data was taken to provide an accurately plotted one-meter contour interval; however, for readability as well as better definition of basic land forms, a fifty centimeter contour interval was interpolated between each even meter both by plotting and visual inspection. Also, the main road crossing each Kom was plotted from centerline data taken by stadia. Hatched lines and spot elevations have been eliminated from the maps published here.

III

THE GEOGRAPHY OF MENDES*

By ROBERT K. HOLZ

Egypt (the Arab Republic of Egypt) is situated at the north-eastern corner of Africa and makes up almost one-thirtieth of the continent's land area. Roughly square in shape, modern Egypt lies between the parallels of 22° and 32° north latitude. Historically the country has been divided into three geographical provinces: 1) the Nile Valley and Delta; 2) the Western Desert, the area west of the Nile, and 3) the Eastern Desert, the area east of the Nile to the Red Sea and the Gulf of Suez. This discussion will be concerned mostly with a division of the province listed first—the Nile Valley and Delta.

The Nile River, a perennial, exotic stream, enters Egypt near Wadi Halfa, some 1,540 kilometers (over 950 miles) south of the northern reaches of the Delta. Along this part of its course the river receives no permanently flowing tributary. It flows through a comparatively narrow valley which has been incised into the almost horizontally-bedded rocks of the Libyan plateau. The excavation of the present river course began in the recent Tertiary by the predecessor of the modern Nile and a great trough[1] was eroded, some four to five hundred meters (1300–1640 feet) deep and ten to fifteen kilometers (six to ten miles) wide. In mid-Pliocene, during a marine transgression, the valley was inundated and filled with sediments. Later, at the beginning of the Pleistocene, these sediments were partially re-excavated. Since the onset of the Pleistocene, which began about a million years ago, the Nile has gone through an alternating series of gravel aggradation and vertical incision with the most recent sediments, some six to eleven meters deep, occupying the center of the valley on either side of the river.

North of Cairo the Nile breaks free of the confining, escarpment-like walls of the limestone trough in which it flows.

Deprived of these lateral restraints, the River spreads out today through its two Delta branches and innumerable distributaries, with only the low rises of the natural levees separating the broad shallow basins.[2] The Nile Delta received its name from Δ, the capital form of the Greek Letter "Delta," and it has become the prototype of all deltas. The Nile Delta is classed as an arcuate type, with an arc-like outer edge, modified by fringing sand spits shaped by marine currents.

A delta is created at the mouth of a river when it empties into the sea or a lake or another slower moving stream. Stream velocity is checked and deposition of the stream load begins. If the tide or other currents cannot remove this deposited material and if the off-shore water is not exceedingly deep, a fan-shaped, gently sloping alluvial tract of new land is formed. Generally, only relatively fine materials make up deltaic deposits, the coarser alluvium having been deposited further up stream. Alluvium deposited in the delta causes the river to divide around it into two or more streams. As the streams subdivide further, they create a triangle or fan-shaped area interlaced by a network of channels. These channels are called distributaries. As the river brings down additional suspended matter, the delta continues to grow laterally and outward, away from the land. Because delta streams are depositing or aggrading, they are actually building new land. The surface of this new land appears flat or level, but in fact it must have a gradient steep enough to allow water to flow, otherwise the delta-forming processes would cease.

From its apex near Cairo to its northern reaches along the Mediterranean littoral the Nile Delta is remarkably flat. A gentle and variable gradient slopes to the north. From Cairo, just south of the Delta head, the Nile drops only about fifty

*The research documented here was made possible, in part, by a grant from the University Research Institute (URI) of The University of Texas at Austin.

1. Karl W. Butzer, "Archaeology and Geology in Ancient Egypt," *Science* 132 (December, 1960), p. 1618.

2. In any flowing stream, velocity is checked by friction along the banks; this is especially true during a flood when water spills out of the normal river channel. Reduced velocity means a decreased capacity for work and some of the suspended stream load is immediately deposited. Repeated occurrence of this phenomenon results in a low mound being built along the side of the stream; it is called a *natural levee.*

feet in elevation along its course to Damietta, a distance of approximately 110 miles. The average gradient along the Damietta branch is less than six inches per mile (less than 1:10,500). In the south, near Cairo, the gradient rises to about 1:6,500, while near the coastal margins it declines to around 1:19,500.

Today the average depth of the alluvial fill of Nilotic silt is estimated at 11.2 meters for the northern Delta and 8.5 meters for the southern Delta. This recent mud overlies a somewhat coarser deposit of sand, silt and fine gravel which is apparently the result of an earlier Holocene filling.[3]

Seismic exploration indicates that the Delta contains at least ten thousand feet of sediments which are poorly consolidated. Such a thick mass of alluvial fill would take a very long time to accumulate, and this could only take place if some subsidence of the earth's crust were associated with it. This most probably resulted from the accumulated weight of the Delta sediments. The exact age of the Delta, however, has not been satisfactorily determined.

The size and shape of the Delta is controlled by the quantity of water and sediments brought down by the Nile and by the level of the Mediterranean. Historical records and geological evidence indicate that the Nile has gone through annual and cyclic variations in stream flow. From Butzer's authoritative work we know that the Mediterranean sea levels have fluctuated considerably in Post-Glacial times.[4] Since the maximum of the Würm Regression (about 20,000 B.C.) there have been at least six different significant levels maintained by the Mediterranean. The most important to this study are: 1) a stage between 4,000 to 3,500 B.C. when sea level stood at four meters above the present level; 2) a decline to minus two-and-a-half meters in about 400 B.C.; 3) a rise to minus two meters by the first century A.D., and 4) the establishment of the present level which occurred in the seventh century, at about the time of the Arab Invasion. When the sea stood at plus four meters, the open sea covered approximately the area of the present littoral lakes, such as Burullus and Menzaleh. Lagoons existed shoreward, but they were limited to the south by the modern three meter contour line—a line which passes well to the north of the Mendes site. It is safe to say that, even at the maximum high stand of the Mediterranean during this period, the Mendes site was still significantly above sea level. The modern Delta lakes were probably formed around A.D. 960 by a rise in sea level which began around the second century A.D. According to Butzer, the Delta has existed in its approximate present dimensions since the last interglacial period;[5] and there seems no doubt that settlement at Mendes first took place on the low rise of a natural levee of an early Delta distributary.

The site of Mendes is divided today into a North and South Kom.[6] Historical, cartographic, as well as visual evidence indicates that these two Koms were once a contiguous landform.[7] They are located in the east-central Nile Delta, four to five miles northeast of es-Simbillâwein and ten to eleven miles southeast of Mansurah which is situated on the eastern bank of the Damietta branch of the Nile. The specific location of the site is longitude 31°32′ east, latitude 30°57′ north.[8]

Both the North and South Koms rise abruptly from the surrounding flat irrigated land of the Delta. They present a steep, escarpment-like slope facing outward, toward the cultivation. In places, erosion and the activities of local cultivators have smoothed the steep sides into a more gentle slope (Plate 33-b). The overall surface of the Koms is irregular and varies considerably in elevation. Although certainly man-made, it resembles the Knob and Kettle moraines of glaciated areas.[9] The highest elevation above sea level on the North Kom (Plate 27-a) is 13.6 meters (forty-four feet) and on the South Kom 10.4 meters (thirty-four feet). The Koms average about thirty feet above the cultivation, although the initial break between the fields and Kom margins is usually from only three to four feet.

As mentioned above, the Delta has a gentle, almost imperceptible gradient which slopes northward. Field measurements and slope analysis, based upon United States Army Map Service topographic sheets at a scale of 1:50,000, indicate a gradient of less than one percent over ninety percent of the area within sixteen miles of the site. The Koms are topographic highs in the almost completely flat Delta landscape. The horizon line is broken by villages, cemeteries and a few widely spaced trees, such as willow, eucalyptus, sycamore, acacia and date palm (Plates 27-b, 29-a, and 33-c).

Vegetation on the Koms is patchy and varies considerably in density. In a few places it may be so thick that the ground surface is hidden (Plate 27-b). Two plant types are dominant upon the Koms. Together they probably make up more than three-fourths of the Kom vegetation. The most common is a coarse bunch grass, much like *Hyparrhenia* (Plate 27-c), known locally by the common name *safsoof*.[10] The plant grows in

3. The Recent or Holocene Epoch of the Quaternary Period is estimated to have begun about 10,000 years ago at the close of the Pleistocene.

4. Karl W. Butzer, "Environment and Human Ecology in Egypt during Predynastic and Early Dynastic Times," *Bulletin de la Société de Géographie d'Egypte* 32 (1959), pp. 56–63.

5. Ibid., p. 59.

6. The North Kom is identified as *Tell el-Rubʿ* or *Tell el-Qasr* on the U.S. Army Map Service *Tell Râk* sheet, Egypt 1:50,000 (Plate 16-d); the South Kom is known as *Tell Timai*. In discussing the ancient Mendesian branch of the Nile, Ball also assigns separate names to these Koms, based on his study of the works of the Classical geographers; John Ball, *Egypt in the Classical Geographers* (Cairo, 1942), p. 27. See also Robert K. Holz, "Man-made Forms in the Nile Delta," *The Geographical Review* LIX, 2 (1969), pp. 253–269.

7. The cultivated area and exposed banks of the irrigation ditches between the Koms abound in pottery sherds and rock fragments. This suggests that agriculture has gradually impinged on the center of the site and divided it into two distinct koms.

8. The location of Mendes on the Survey of Egypt grid, using the Helmert Spheroid, is about 914 North and 664 East. On the 1,000 Meter Universal Transverse Mercator Grid, Zone 36, International Spheroid, the location would be approximately UV58126.

9. Knob and Kettle moraines are ridge-like landforms deposited at the terminus of a glacier when it is at a standstill. The moraine surface is rough and irregular with pits or depressions (Kettles) and hills (Knobs); Arthur Strahler, *Physical Geography* (New York, 1960), pp. 400–401.

10. Vivi and Gunnar Täckholm, *The Flora of Egypt* I (Cairo, 1941), pp. 142–143.

thick clumps reaching a height of two to three feet (Plate 27-b, foreground). Ordinarily the bunches grow three to four feet apart, but in a few places they are so closely spaced that the bending spikelets of opposing plants become interwoven, providing an extremely dense ground cover. The other dominant species is *Alhagi maurorum* or camel thorn (Plate 27-d). Locally the plant is known by its common name *Aqool* (*Aqoul*).[11]

Vegetation tends to be concentrated toward the outer and lower edges of the Koms. The higher interiors are almost bare. This is a result of deficient precipitation, heavy salt concentrations, and/or impermeable subsurface layers which stop the upward capillary movement of water.

Climatic data for the Nile Delta are sparse, inadequate and difficult to obtain, the modern continuance records having been kept for only short periods.[12] The weather station closest to the Mendes site is at Mansurah, and the climatic figures for this station will be used in the following discussion.[13]

Climatically the Nile Delta is classed as a hot desert, or *BWh*, according to the Koppen-Geiger empirical quantitative system of climatic classification.[14] The Mendes region has an average annual temperature of 70.2° F., with precipitation concentrated in winter and early spring. On the basis of this temperature figure and the time and amount of precipitation, a minimum of 432 mm. (seventeen inches) of rainfall would be required for the area to be classified as *BSh* or Steppe (short grassland) climate. As the Mendes region receives an average yearly precipitation of only fifty-five millimeters (2.17 inches) at Mansurah, it is considerably less than the amount needed for steppe classification. Climatically then, although the irrigated cultivation does not reflect it, Mendes is a desert.

Despite low rainfall, atmospheric humidity is high. Even in summer, during the hottest part of the day, the relative humidity may range from a low of thirty to thirty-five per cent to a high approaching one hundred per cent at night when the air cools below the dew point. In the morning, dense fog and heavy dew are common throughout the Delta. The fog is sometimes not dissipated until ten or eleven o'clock. The humidity is the result of air masses which originate over the Mediterranean and are carried inland by the prevailing north wind. Little rainfall is produced because the air masses warm up as they move inland and precipitation triggering devices are lacking. The flatness and low elevation of the Nile Delta provide no barrier to the southward advance of Mediterranean air masses. For example, around Mendes, thirty-four or thirty-five miles from the sea, the elevation averages only three-and-a-half to four meters (twelve to fourteen feet) above sea level. The precipitation which does fall is concentrated in the three

winter months; thirty millimeters (1.18 inches) or about fifty-five percent of the total falls then. June, July, August, and September, the growing season in Egypt, show no rainfall in their monthly averages. Normally rainfall begins in late October, and at Mansurah monthly averages increase to a maximum of slightly more than one-half inch (0.51 in.; 13 mm.) in January. The monthly precipitation averages show a decline to early May which has an average of three millimeters (0.12 inches). Even though this is an arid climate, high atmospheric humidity and cooler winter temperature retard evaporation, so that, for days after a winter or late spring rain, the Mendes area may become a muddy morass.

Temperatures in the Delta are relatively high all year. However, there is a distinct winter season which is shown by a January average of 56.1° F., as compared with July and August averages of 82° F. There is a yearly range of 25.9° F. between the average of the monthly summer high and the monthly winter high temperatures. Summer high daily temperatures are ameliorated by the north wind, by morning clouds and fog. Normal daytime highs average 90° to 93° F. Rarely does the air temperature reach 100° F., unless readings are taken in a sheltered place, away from the prevailing north wind. Summer nighttime temperatures average 70° to 74° F. Winter daytime highs average 60° to 65° F., with nighttime lows of 40° to 45° F. Freezing temperatures are not common, but every eight or ten years they may occur.

The Mendes area has an average potential evapo-transpiration of 1121 mm. (44.1 inches) per year, but, with an annual average precipitation of only fifty-five millimeters, there is a yearly water deficit of 1066 mm. (41.9 inches).[15] Moreover, during the growing season when no precipitation occurs, there is a complete soil moisture deficit unless water is supplied by irrigation. The summer climate of the Mendes area may be described as hot and humid, without rainfall, winter as mild and humid, with occasional rain.

The depth of the ground water table in this area of the Delta varies considerably, both annually and with the season.[16] From late summer to early fall, when the inundation is in progress, the water table rises above the surfaces of some of the low lying fields and flooding results. Just before the annual flood begins, the water table lies at its lowest level below the ground surface. Depending on the amount of water brought down by the Nile, this varies from one summer to the next. The depth of the water table also varies locally, depending on the proximity to the branches of the Nile, its distributaries or major canals. During the time of low water, the water table may lie from

11. Vivi and Gunnar Täckholm, op. cit. III (Cairo, 1954), pp. 213–214.

12. J. M. J. Coutelle, "Observations météorologiques, faites au Kaire en 1799, 1800 et 1801," and "Observations sur les variations horaires du baromêtre," in *Description de l'Egypte* XIX (Paris, 1824), pp. 451–466. These are some of the early references, but they are brief and incomplete.

13. The Ministry of War and Marine, Meteorological Department, Climate Section, *Climatological Normal for Egypt* (Cairo, 1950).

14. Arthur Strahler, op. cit., pp. 186–187.

15. C. W. Thornwaite Associates, *Average Climatic Water Balance Data of the Continents*, Part I. *Africa* XV (Centerton, N. J., 1962), p. 284.

16. The ground water table is that zone of the soil which is naturally saturated with water (zone of saturation or phreatic zone). It is that part in which all the voids or interstices between the soil particles are filled with water. The water table is separated from the ground surface by the *zone of aeration*, or the *vadose zone*, through which water may move upward or downward, depending on moisture conditions at the surface. For a more complete discussion, see James H. Zumberge, *Elements of Geology* (New York, 1963), p. 127.

ten to fifteen feet below the surface. Throughout the rest of the year it averages from three to five feet in depth. This is the result of the gentle Delta gradient, low elevation and extensive water distribution within the cultivation. Because the depth of the ground water table conforms rather closely to the surface topography, it would be expected that the table would lie at a higher level under the Koms which are topographic highs on the landscape. In fact this does occur and several of the excavation pits at Mendes have penetrated it.

On the Koms, water is not available in sufficient quantity to flush the salts from the soil. Run-off is collected into ponds in the basins on the surface of the Koms. Evaporation leaves the solutional salts behind, concentrating them near or at the surface where they may form a light crust.[17] The bottom of some of these basins contains a non-permeable layer of mud brick, fired brick, or stone, which may mark the foundations of ancient buildings or, as in one basin at Tell el Rub‘a, the floor of the so-called Sacred Lake (Plate 34-d), which was deliberately sealed to hold water.

To the southeast and east of Mendes are two distinctive landforms which, while not directly connected with or related to the ancient site, are important in understanding its general historical and geographic relationships within the Delta. The first, to the southeast, is a great sand ridge known as a *turtle back*. It is located near the village of Sangaha (Plate 13-a), eight or nine miles southeast of the South Kom. Roughly elliptical in shape, with a long north-south axis, it is composed of fine to coarse fluviatile sands. These sands were deposited in the head or apex of the eastern and central parts of the Delta during some former period of higher Mediterranean sea level. Rapidly decreasing sea levels during the late Upper Pleistocene caused the degradation of the Nile. Steep channels were cut into the older sand deposits so quickly that there was little time or energy for lateral erosion. Today the remnants of these older deposits stand up as distinct landforms or turtle backs between the Delta distributaries. They rise well above the alluvium—the one near Sangaha is from twenty-five to thirty feet above the cultivation. They provided sites for early settlements, cult places and cemeteries, safely above the annual flood level.

The other landform to the east (Plate 27-e), is a narrow ridge, twelve to twenty-five feet high, extending from east to west for about four and one-half miles.[18] The western end of this landform begins about four miles east of the North Kom just east of Ghurûr (Plate 15-c). It is composed of Delta alluvium and shows no evidence of ancient occupation. The long east-west trending ridge, known as Tell el Qimân (Tell el Qenan) and located to the east of Tell el Rub‘a (Plate 13-a), is probably the remains of the spoil pile excavated from the channel of the ancient Butic River. The earth was thrown up on the south side of the stream to form a mound which would retain the Nile floodwaters on the lands to the south.[19] About three and one-half miles east of Tell el Rub‘a the ridge angles rather suddenly to the southwest. If a straight line is drawn along this angle on a map, it passes between the North and South Koms. Furthermore, the major and supplementary contour lines in this area also lead towards the cultivated space between the Koms, which is topographically lower than the Koms themselves. These contour lines, which generally run parallel to the ridge, suggest that it may have separated the sites in historic times. While the ridge is still a distinctive landform on the Delta plain, no evidence of the former Butic River channel remains. Ptolemy mentions the Butic River, and its course may be observed in Plate 2-c, -d. It ran supposedly from east to west, parallel to the coast.[20]

---

17. All so-called "fresh" water running over the surface of the earth contains dissolved salts. These come from the natural chemical weathering of the earth's rocks. In general, streams in arid regions contain a higher level of dissolved salts per given quantity of water. In arid and semi-arid climates, where runoff is concentrated in shallow basins forming temporary or ephemeral ponds, as the water evaporates the salts are concentrated at the surface of the lake bed. The result after evaporation is a landform known as a *salt pan* or *salina*.

18. The author and several other members of the Mendes Expedition investigated this landform during the summer of 1965. No pottery sherds, rock fragments, remnants of buildings, or other signs of ancient occupancy were observed. However, several recent Moslem cemeteries have been placed there, undoubtedly to keep the interred above the inundation. A modern village, Ez. Abd el Salam, or part of it, is located on the landform. See also Plate 13-a and Page 12 above.

19. Ball, op. cit., p. 129, footnote 4, also refers to the landform which, however, has been noted since the French Expedition; see for instance Jomard, *Description de l'Egypte* IX (Paris, 1829), p. 375 (*Mendes* II, P. 43); J. F. Michaud, *Correspondence d'Orient* VI (Paris, 1831), p. 324; and Linant de Bellefonds, "Carte de l'Isthme de Suez Ancienne" in his *Mémoire sur les principaux travaux d'utilité publique exécutés en Egypte* (Paris, 1873).

20. Ball, op. cit., p. 129; Bietak, *Tell el-Dab‘a* II, pp. 92–93.

IV

MENDES TODAY

A. TELL EL RUB'A (North Kom)

By DONALD P. HANSEN and DAVID STIEGLITZ

The mound of Tell el Rub'a lies seventeen kilometers southeast of Mansurah, capital of Daqahaliya Province, and about one kilometer west of the village of El Rub'a (Plate 28). The mound[1] has an approximate north-south longitudinal axis, and a perimeter of about five and a half kilometers. In its greatest dimensions it measures 1.58 kilometers in length and 0.84 kilometers in width. In antiquity the Tell must have covered a larger area, for there is evidence that the surrounding fields have encroached on all sides. As mentioned in the previous chapter, the highest point on the mound is approximately twenty meters above sea level and about sixteen meters above the level of the plain. The height of the Tell at its edge varies from four to seven meters above sea level. As a convenience in describing the mound, it may be divided into four basic parts: The Temple Precinct, The North Tip, Tell el 'Izam and its environs, and The Southern Mound.

The Temple Precinct

At present the most distinctive feature of Tell el Rub'a is the large mudbrick wall around the Temple Precinct (Plates 27-a, 29-a) enclosing an area of approximately twenty hectares or fifty acres (N 500—S 200, W 300—E 200). There are extreme variations in the present height of the wall and in its state of preservation. The average height is probably six meters above ground level, while the greatest height is about thirteen meters at the south end of the east wall. Because of natural erosion and excavation, the wall in cross section has a triangular shape. It is apparent in the west that the bottom of the foundation rests on what is now the surface of the Tell (Plate 29-b). Hence we must conclude that the major part of the preserved wall is only foundation and that enormous amounts of debris from the original wall have been carted away from the Precinct

area. At no point is the original thickness of the wall ascertainable without excavation.

The Enclosure Wall[2] is readily visible on the east and west. Two small openings, one on each side, approximately ten meters wide, may well have been gates into the Precinct (Plates 18, 29-a). In the south, buildings once abutted on the wall. Because of large cuts below the foundation level, especially at the southern end of the west wall (N 20—N 180), it is almost impossible to make a distinction between the debris and the wall line itself. Along the north wall a cut of two hundred meters (between W 5 and E 150) presents the same difficulty. In the northwest corner of the Precinct, a smaller precinct was apparently formed by a perpendicular extension of the west wall (Plate 19). The bounded area, which is very flat, covers approximately one hectare (N 400–500, W 00–100) (Plate 29-c, -d).

Located near the geometric center of the Temple Precinct is a slight rise, roughly rectangular in shape (N 150—S 20, W 50—W 150) (Plates 19 and 30-a). This is clearly the area of a temple. Its longitudinal orientation is basically the same as that of the enclosure walls. The longitudinal axis of both deviates from the True North by 21°20' E. The rise is dominated by the great granite Naos, inscribed by Amasis, in the southern extremity of the sanctuary (Plates 1 and 30). The monolith rests on a large granite base below which are several courses of limestone. Numerous granite and limestone blocks were strewn about the depression surrounding the Naos (Plate 30-c). Immediately to the west and the south of the Naos, part of the mudbrick temple foundations are visible (Plate 30-d). Extensive quarrying has distributed granite, limestone, and quartzite chips over the entire surface of the sanctuary area (Plate 30-e). In addition, there are also a few large inscribed blocks.

On the west side, well below the level of the sanctuary, in an area where the *sebbakhin* have cut extensively into the

---

1. Plates 17–21.

2. It has recently been discussed by G. R. H. Wright in *ZDPV* 84 (1968), p. 14.

mound, a white limestone tomb belonging to Tety-ishetef was exposed in 1907 (N 133—W 133) (Plate 31-a). The inscription was recorded by Chabân and, although now completely empty, the burial chamber is still preserved.[3]

To the north of the Temple Area, remains of quarrying and large architectural stone fragments indicate the emplacement of a second structure with a completely different orientation (N 220–290, W 60–108) (Plate 31-b).

To the west of the Temple Area is a relatively flat space with numerous fragments of black granite ram sarcophagi. The fragments cluster into two main groups. The southern group is located at N 12–25, W 266–295 (Plate 31-c; *Mendes* II, Pl. 1-b), and lies in a depression formed by the conjectural portion of the south Enclosure Wall and a small mound to the north which itself is severely trenched through the middle. The northern group is located at N 260–295, W 120–150, on a flat area extending north from the small mound (Plate 31-d). A few fragments of other sarcophagi are scattered between these two groups. The only inscribed ram sarcophagus from Tell el Rub'a is now in the Cairo Museum.[4]

The highest preserved portion within the Precinct is situated against the east Enclosure Wall (Plate 27-a); parts of this area, like the rest of the mound, have been badly gutted. The architectural remains are covered with a heavy deposit of pot sherds. The area is divided into two by a depression which leads to the apparent gate in the east wall (Plate 32-b). In the northern part are five inscribed blocks[5] on the surface near N 350—E 150 (Plate 32-c), and in the southern part is a giant sarcophagus composed of a black granite box within a white limestone casing (N 40—E 60) (Plate 32-d). This is the sarcophagus in which in 1869 Daninos found the lower part of a shawabti of King Nepherites of Dynasty XXIX (see *Mendes* II, Pp. 92, 203, **97**, and Pl. 29-e to -g).[6]

To the south of the Great Naos there has been extensive digging by the *sebbakhin* in buildings which have the character of private houses (Plate 33-a). Beyond this the mound descends abruptly to the southern plain as though it had recently been cut away. A similar leveling of the edge of the mound, probable recent, may be observed at the southern tip (Plate 33-b).

The Northern Tip

The rather flat area running south-north through the middle of the Precinct extends into the Northern Tip of the Kom. Although on the whole flat, a rise at the center of the Northern Tip reveals baked bricks and therefore evidence of buildings. At the extreme end of the mound is a contemporary *ezbah* or

farm (Plates 32-a, 33-c). To the west lie three Ramesside stone fragments originally part of a single block (N 550, W 00–10) (Plate 33-d; *Mendes* II, Pl. 10-a to -c).[7] It is impossible to tell whether they belonged to an architectural structure elsewhere. Further to the west is Mendes House built for the Expedition.

Tell el 'Izam

To the east of the east Enclosure Wall, and separated from it by a deep north-south depression, lies the mound called Tell el 'Izam (Plates 20 and 34-a) within the coordinates N 100–300, E 250–380. To the north and south of this mound are flat, roughly rectangular depressions, both of which are partially bounded by mudbrick walls (Plate 34-b). The mound is composed of pure sand and very sandy soil. Without excavation it is impossible to ascertain whether the sand is a natural geological deposit or was brought in from the outside. The surface is littered with bone fragments, and on the south there are large hunks of a vitrified substance with bone imbedded in it. On the east the mound slopes evenly down to the fields.[8]

A flat depression on a level with the fields to the east separates Tell el 'Izam and its environs from the Southern Mound. This depression is like a large and rectangular field.

The Southern Mound

The Southern Mound is bounded on the north by a ridge (E 160–360), apparently formed of architectural remains, running perpendicular to the east Enclosure Wall (Plates 20 and 34-c). West and slightly south of the ridge is a roughly rectangular depression abutting on the east Enclosure Wall where it steps west and then south (Plate 34-d). This depression is nearly flat and in Pharaonic times may well have been the Sacred Lake. The Southern Mound is bisected by a wide strip of scrub, cutting from S 400–600 in the west, up to S 200–400 in the east (Plate 35-a). Except for a small kiln, this area has no distinguishing features. Various architectural remains extend both north and south of it (Plate 35-b). In the area to the north, mudbrick walls stand to a considerable height and there are several large pits, while in the area to the south a mound rises near its southern tip (S 700–800, E 250–350) (Plate 35-c). The brick and limestone architectural remains here may once have formed public buildings. The red-colored soil and vitrified brick provide evidence of extensive burning during the last phase of occupation. The sharp drop of the mound at this point again indicates that originally the Southern Mound extended further south (Plate 33-b), which may or may not mean that Tell el Rub'a and Tell Timai were at one time connected.[9]

---

3. *Mendes* II, P. 191, **6**, and Pls. 6-c, 9-c, -d.
4. *Mendes* II, P. 213, **163**, and Pl. 38-a.
5. *Mendes* II, Pp. 191, **4**, 192, **11–14**; and Pl. 9-a.
6. This is the sarcophagus referred to in *MDIK* 27 (1971), p. 121, note 51, where the author has confused the southern part of the Temple Precinct of the North Kom, Tell el Rub'a, with the South Kom, Tell Timai.

7. *Mendes* II, P. 192, **8–10**.
8. *Mendes* II, P. 17.
9. However, see above Page viii.

MENDES TODAY

B. TELL TIMAI (South Kom)

By EDWARD OCHSENSCHLAGER

The northern edge of Tell Timai lies approximately one-half kilometer to the south of Tell el Rub'a. In the northwestern part, the mound (Plates 22–26) is partially covered by the modern village of Kafr el Amir Abdallah Sheikh Ibn es-Salam or, for short, Kafr el Amir, and its cemetery (Plates 37-a and 40-c). As Timai el Amdid, the village which takes its name from Tell Timai, lies well to the east of the Kom, it does not appear on the new map of Mendes (Plate 17), but may be seen in the distance on Plate 39-c. Tell Timai is larger than Tell el Rub'a; its perimeter amounts to about seven kilometers, covering over two hundred acres (Plate 36). Its highest point, approximately 18.5 meters above sea level, is located near the topographic center of the mound. Most of the mound slopes evenly from the center down to the surrounding fields where it measures less than seven meters above sea level. There is at present no definite indication that the Kom extended north and joined Tell el Rub'a, but see above, Pp. viii, 20 (Note 7), and 24.

The Central Section

The Central Section of the mound (S 1800–2250, W 400—E 350), lying deep below the general surface, has the appearance of a burned-out city; Hellenistic buildings and parts of buildings stand to a considerable height (Plate 37-b), and there is evidence of streets running through them (Plate 37-c). Although most of the remains were probably at one time private buildings, some large-scale structures were obviously public buildings. Besides enormous layered deposits of sherds among the ruins, there are stone architectural fragments, as well as traces of wall paintings and mosaic floors. Some of the building remains now visible may have been foundations. Others, with openings for windows, doors and wooden beams, were living walls (Plate 38-a, -b), several of which retain portions of a second story. Most of the destruction of the Central Section seems to have been done fairly recently by the *sebbakhin*.

The Northern Section

This area (S 1400–1800, W 100—E 200) has a large central depression from which not long ago ancient buildings were completely removed (Plate 38-c). The embankment of the narrow gauge railroad built in 1913 borders the depression on the northeast. On the east it is bounded by a long low rise, and on the south and west by a sharp rise where earth removal ceased. On the west the earth removal exposed a limestone platform approximately 10 × 10 meters (Plate 38-c, -d), two sarcophagus fragments[1] (Plate 39-a), a sarcophagus lid[2] and a limestone sphinx (Plate 39-b). From the southern ridge a characteristic slope rises to the gutted remains in the center of the mound.

The Eastern Extension

The Eastern Extension of the Kom (S 1700–2000, E 200–900) is relatively flat. The only distinguishing features are two irregular mounds, the remains of brick kilns (S 1910–1955, E 335–450). The tops of the kilns are between twelve and thirteen meters above sea level and rise about 4.5 meters above the surrounding area (Plate 39-c). Near the eastern end of the Eastern Extension the remains of a large structure in fired brick may be the "Koronfich" on Daressy's sketch plan (*Mendes* II, P. 105, Croquis IV), photographed during Langsdorff and Schott's visit in 1930 (*Mendes* II, Pl. 7-b).

The Southeast Quarter

A general rise to the south (S 2000–2600, E 350–700) reveals a north-south band of badly destroyed architectural remains (Plate 40-a), including fired brick, mudbrick, and stone frag-

1. Through the kindness of the late Mr. Alexandre Lézine, son-in-law of the late Pierre Montet, who visited Mendes between March 19 and 22, 1947, we received copies of the sketches which he made at that time of both fragments (which may actually belong to the same sarcophagus) labeled "NAOS" in the illustration on the next page.

2. The lid, incidentally, was no longer there in 1963.

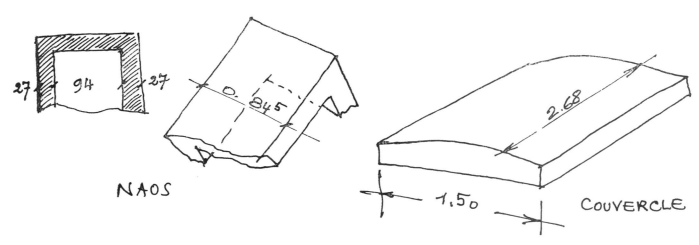

Tell Timai, Northern Section: sarcophagus fragments and lid (drawing by A. Lézine).

ments, with vitrified brick debris which may well come from another kiln.

The South Area

This is the largest flat area on either Kom (S 2100–2600, E 350—W 100) and has few distinguishing features except that, at the south, it drops off sharply to the fields. Baked brick, vitrified materials, and stone architectural fragments are distributed at random over the surface, among them fragments of monolithic columns and fluted column drums. One group of columns includes a badly worn granite Corinthian capital (Plate 39-d); another group consists of monolithic columns in red granite (Plate 40-b).

The Southwest Area

West of the flat area, the terrain (S 2100–2550, W 100–600) is pitted and covered with a heavy scattering of vitrified material (Plate 40-c). Further to the southwest the mound is less pitted; it lacks the vitrified material, but a few stone architectural fragments are scattered about on the surface. Again there is a steep drop to the southern fields, with a gradual drop to the west.

PLATES

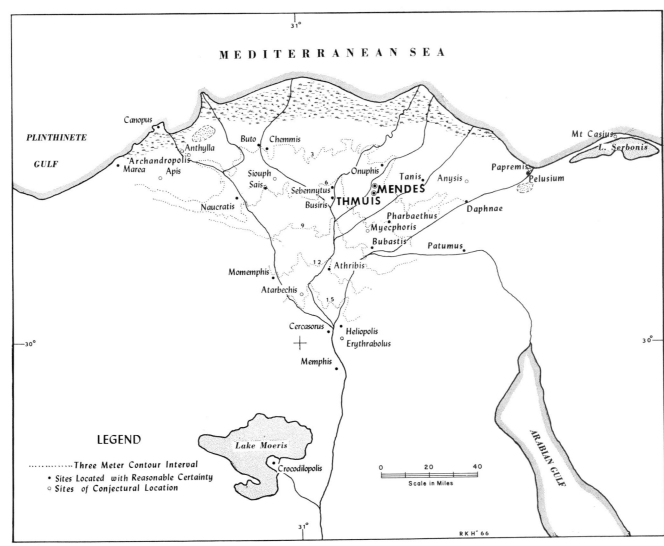

a   According to Herodotus   C. 450 B.C.

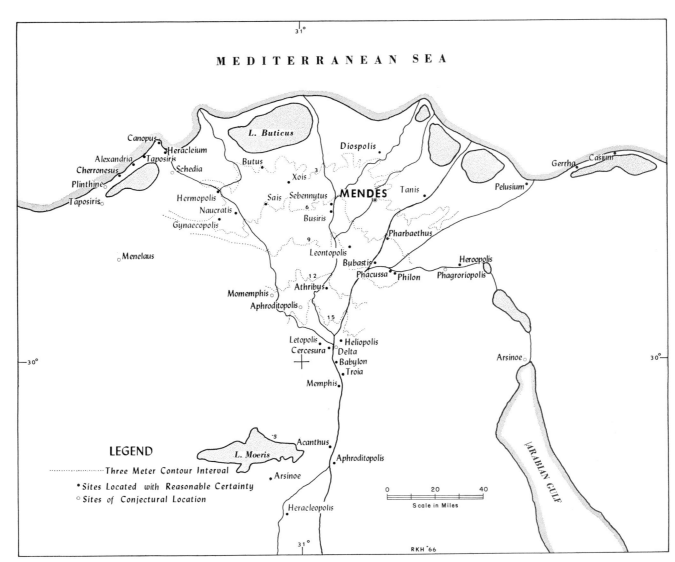

b   According to Strabo   C. 20 B.C.

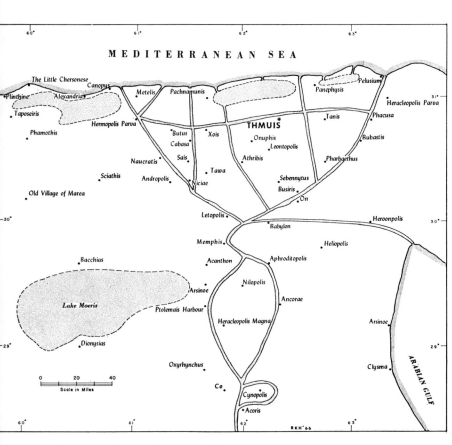

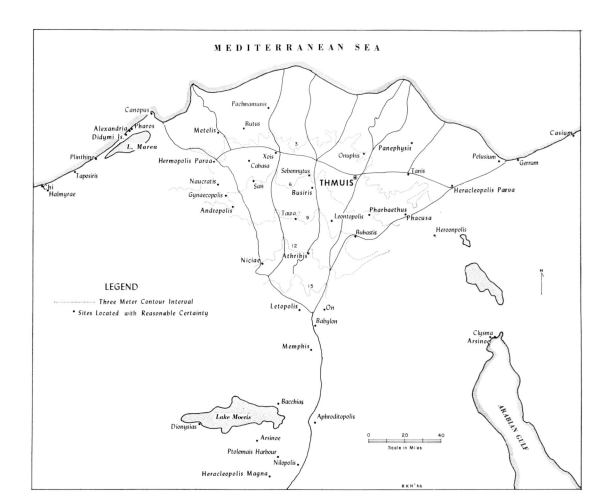

According to Ptolemy the Geographer   c. A.D. 150   d   With Ptolemy's Names in Place

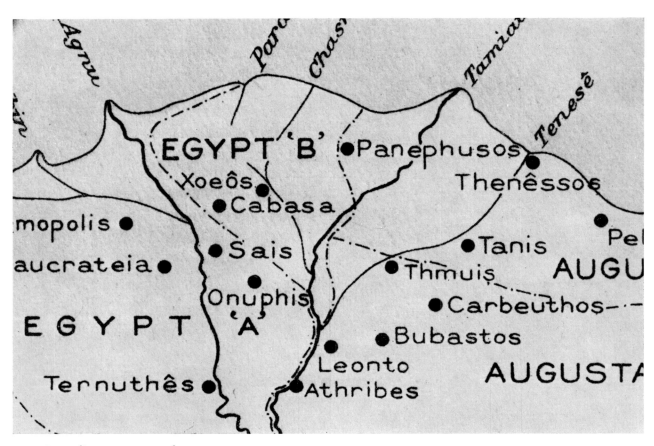

e   According to George of Cyprus   A.D. 606

PLATE 3   Earliest Maps of the Nile Delta

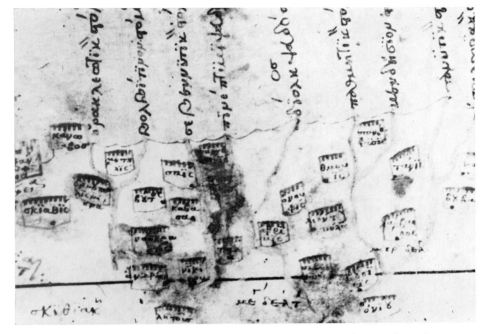

a   Codex Urbinas Graecus 82 (Ms.)   Late 12th or early 13th century

b   Codex Vaticanus Latinas 5698 (Ms.)   Early 15th century

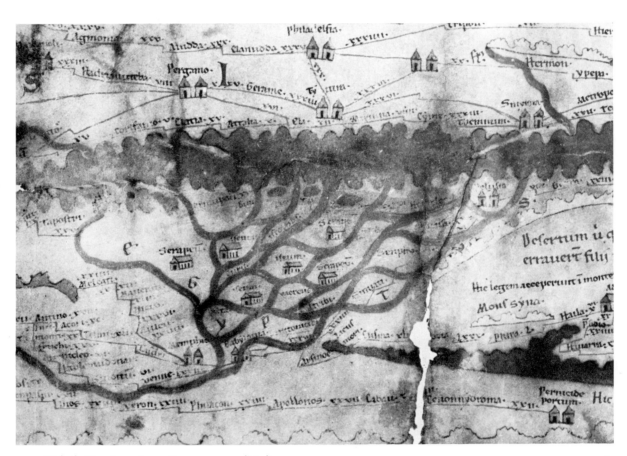

c   Tabula Peutingeriana, Segment VIII (Ms.)   1265

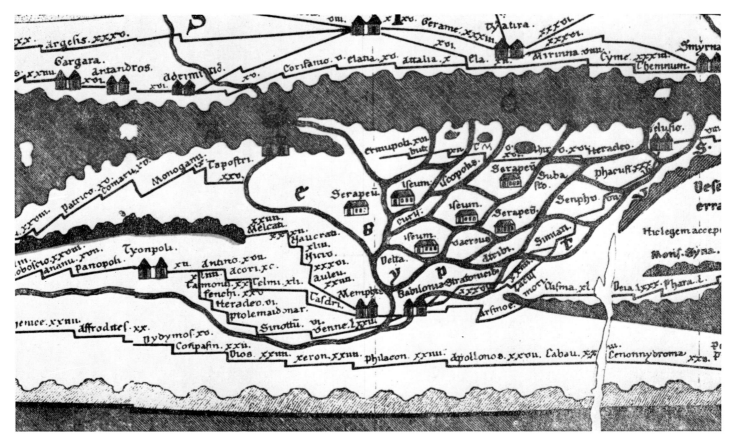

d   Tabula Peutingeriana, Segment VIII (modern copy)

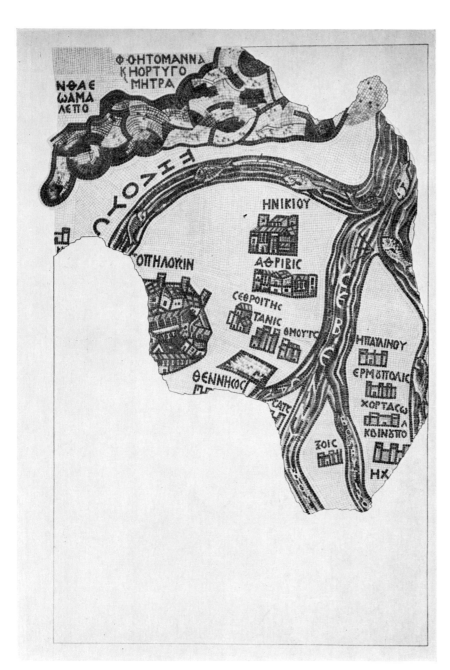

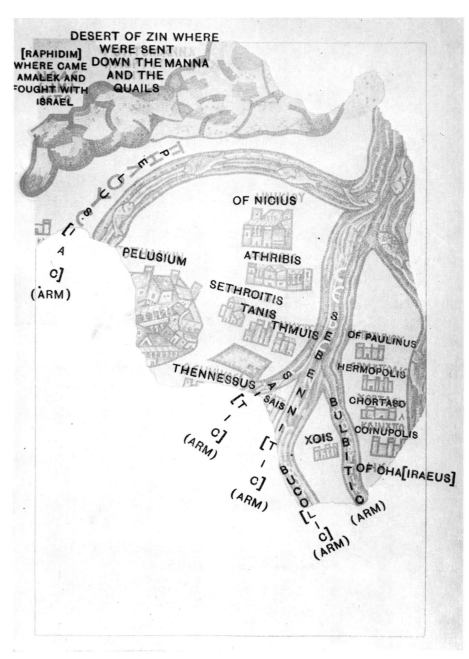

e   Madaba Mosaic Map   A.D. 560–565   f   Madaba Mosaic Map (modern copy)

PLATE 4 Earliest Printed Maps of the Nile Delta

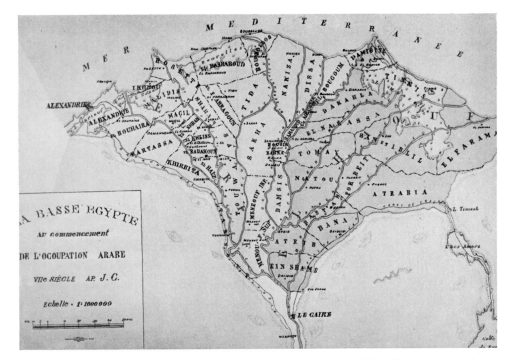

a *La Basse Egypte* (historical map, with Arab designations of the 7th century A.D.)

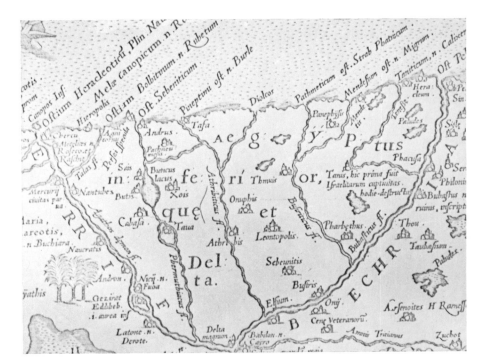

b Ortelius, *Aegyptus Antiquus* 1565

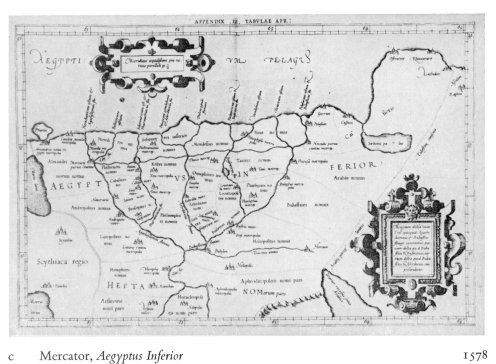

c Mercator, *Aegyptus Inferior* 1578

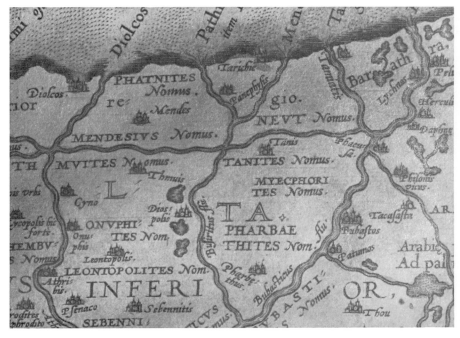

d Ortelius, *Aegyptus Antiquus* 1584

a   Thronos Alexandrinos (Ms. of the 17th century)   7th-8th Century

b   Tavernier, *Patriarchatus Alexandrini*   1640

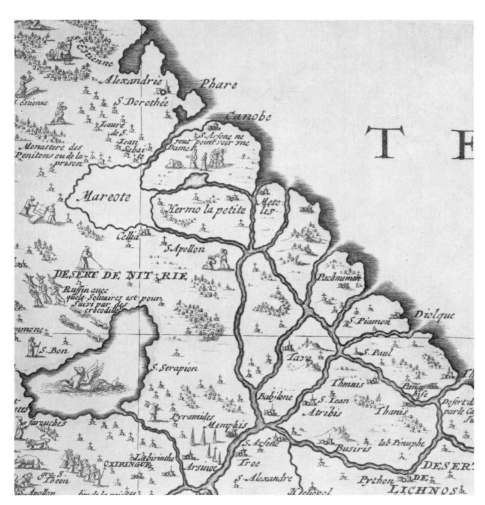

c   Michalet, *Les Deserts d'Egypte*   1693

d   Sanson, *Aegyptus Antiqua*   1705

e   Duval, *Aegyptus Antiqua*   1710 (?)

PLATE 6 French Maps of the 18th Century

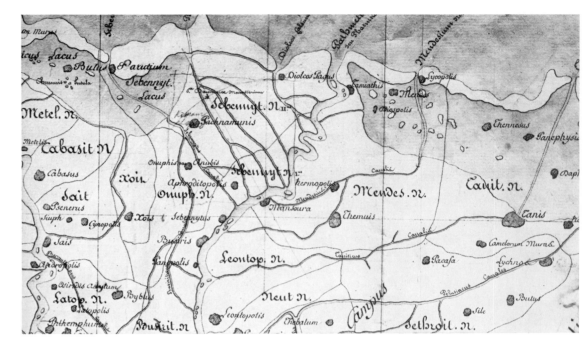

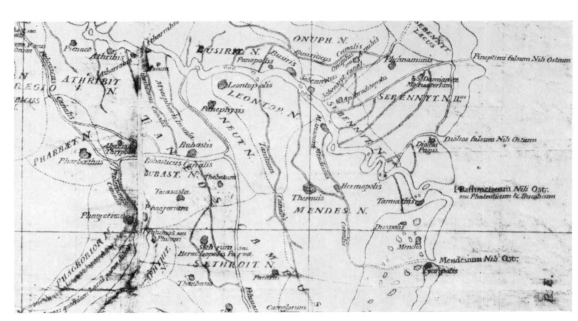

a   Lucas, *Carte de la Basse Egypte*   1717

c   D'Anville, *Carte de l'Egypte ancienne* (Ms.)   c. 1729

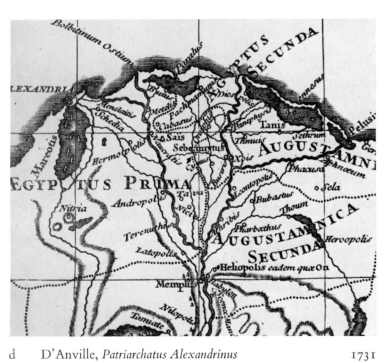

d   D'Anville, *Patriarchatus Alexandrinus*   1731

e   D'Anville, *Egypte nommée dans le pays Missir*   1750

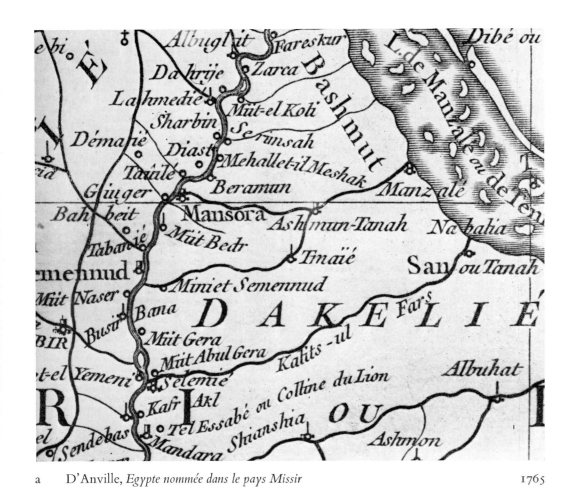

a   D'Anville, *Egypte nommée dans le pays Missir*   1765

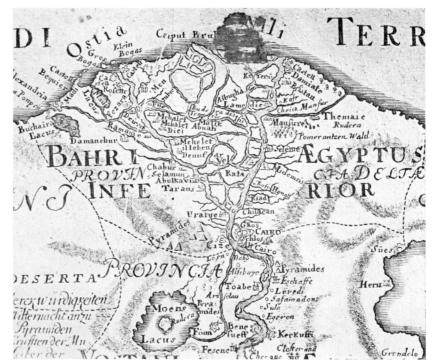

b   Homann, *Aegyptus Hodierna*   1731

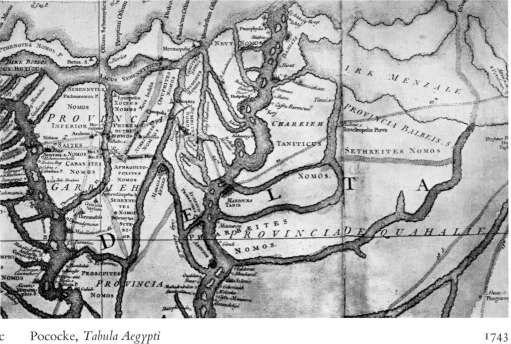

c   Pococke, *Tabula Aegypti*   1743

d   Vaugondy, *Carte de l'Egypte ancienne et moderne*   1753

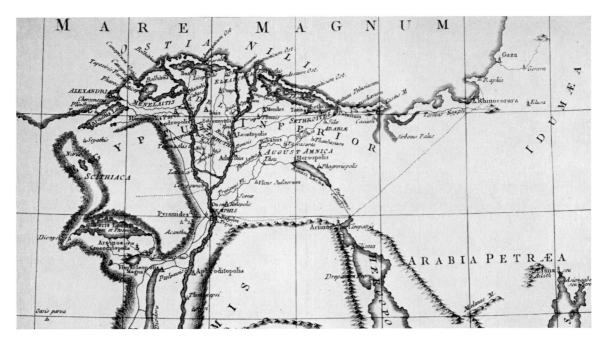

e   Bonne, *Aegyptus*   1786

PLATE 8   Maps from the End of the 18th Century

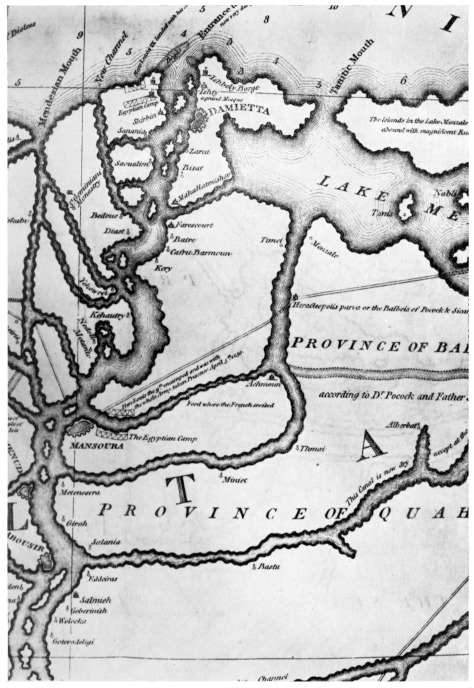

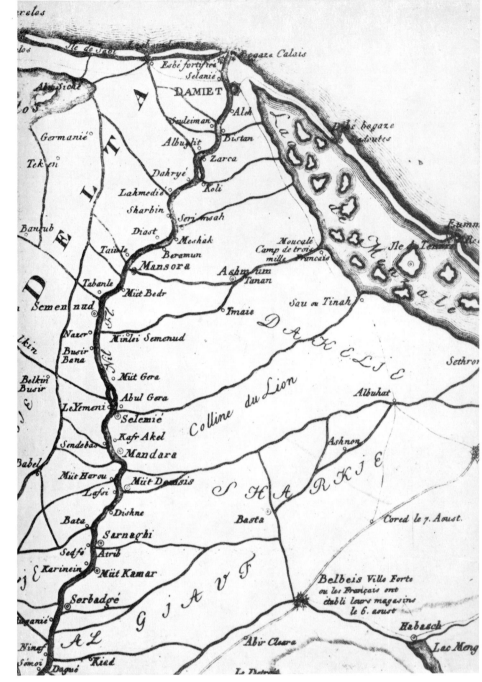

a   Heather, *A New Plan of Egypt*   1798

b   Kauffer, *Carte de l'Egypte*   1799

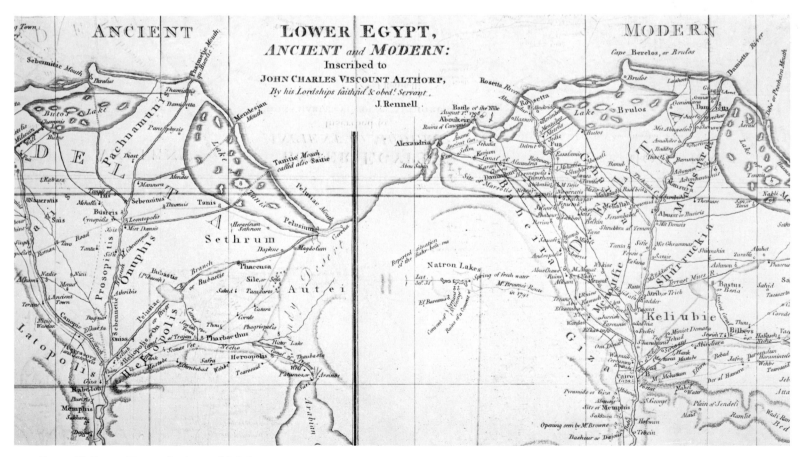

c   Rennell, *Lower Egypt, Ancient and Modern*   1799

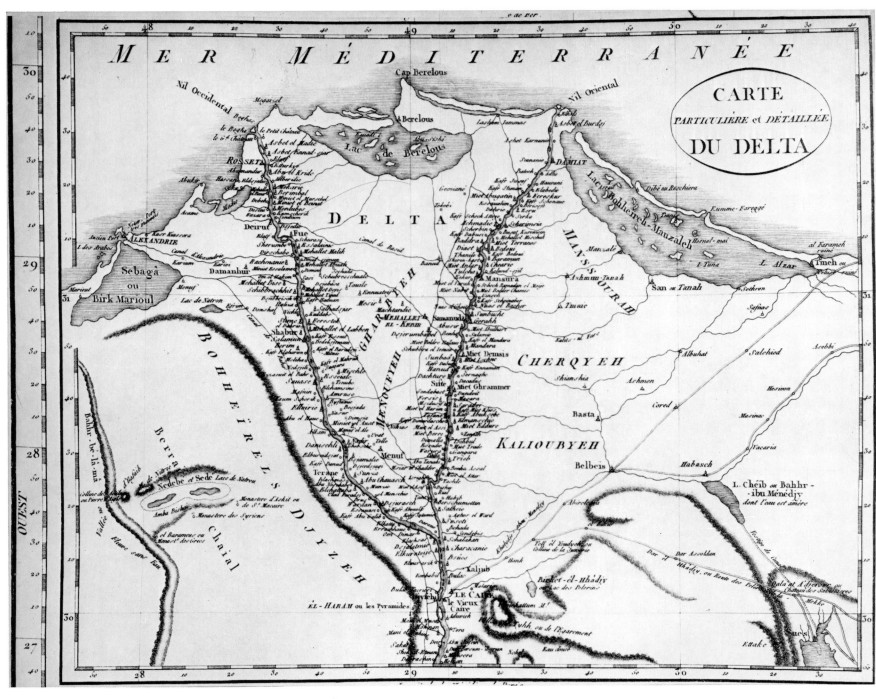

d   Mentelle and Chanlaire, *Carte Physique et Politique de l'Egypte*   1799

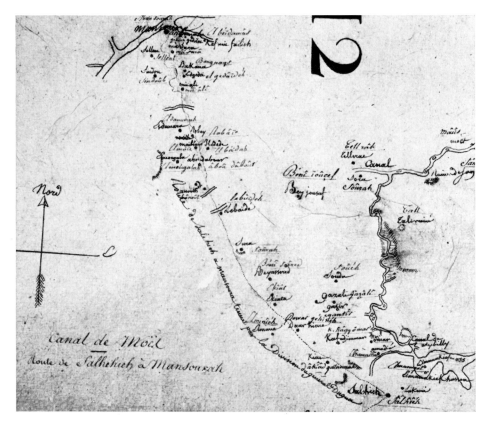

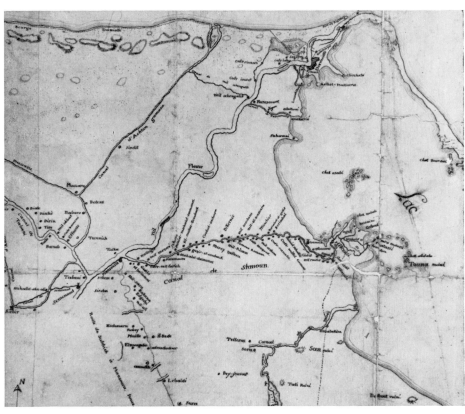

e   *Canal de Moël. Route de Salhehieh à Mansourah* (Ms. version)   1799   f   *CARTE d'une partie de la basse-EGYPTE;* La route de Salehieh (printed version)

a   *Carte hydrographique* (*Description, Etat Moderne* I)   1800

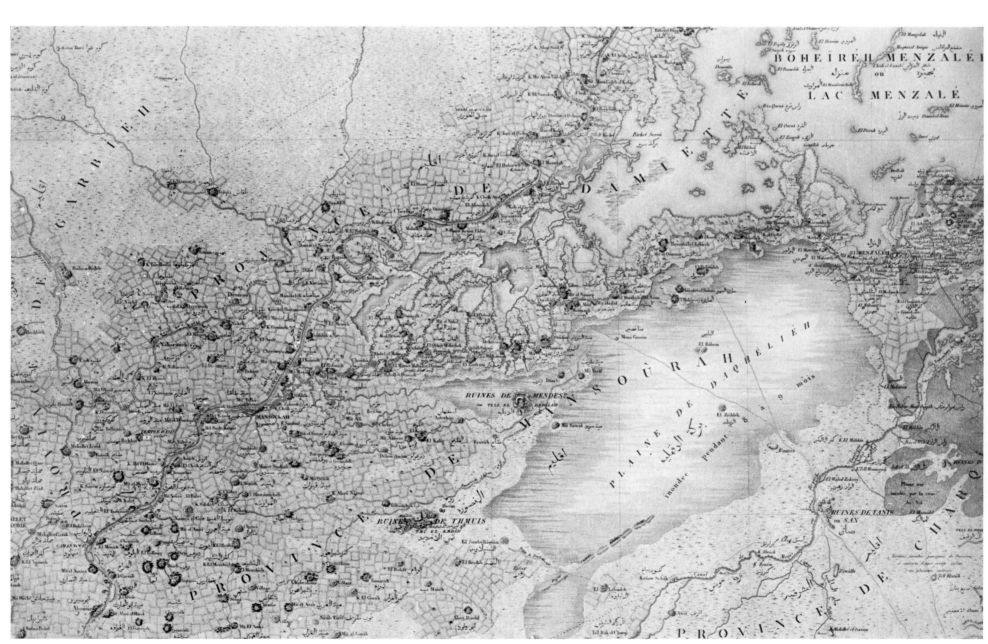

b   *Mansoûrâh, Sân* (*Description, Atlas, Feuille 35*)   1800

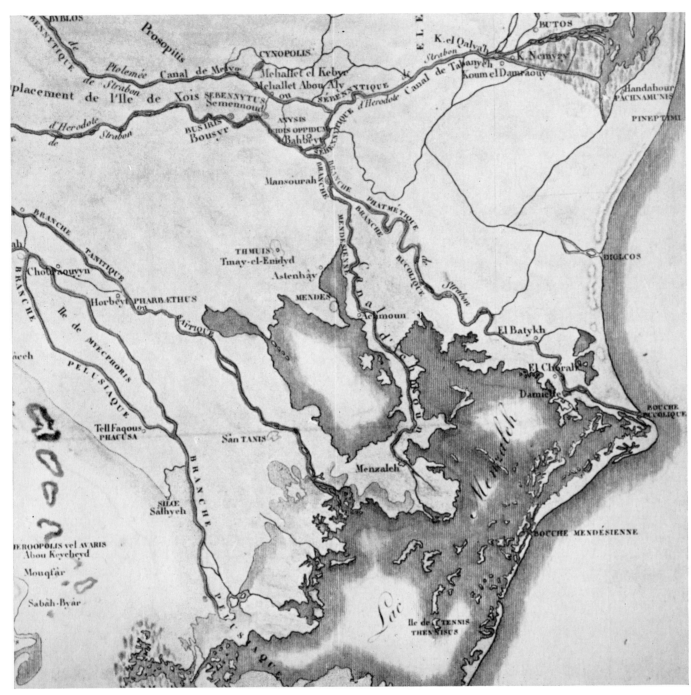

c   *Les anciennes branches du Nil* (*Description, Antiquités* VIII)   1800

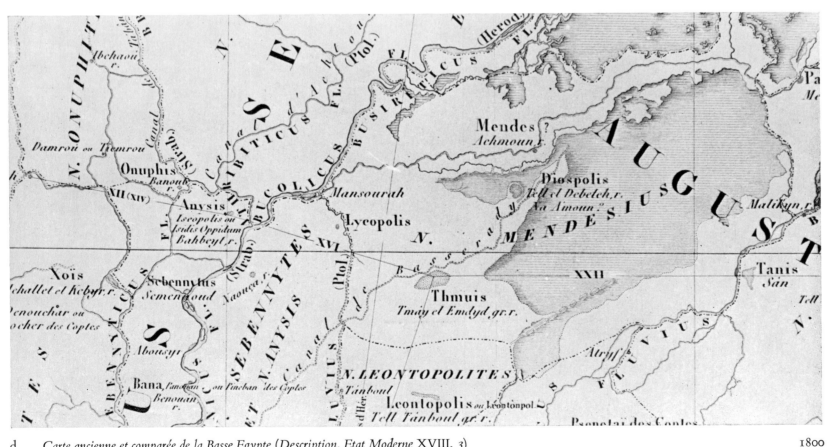

d   *Carte ancienne et comparée de la Basse Egypte* (*Description, Etat Moderne* XVIII, 3)   1800

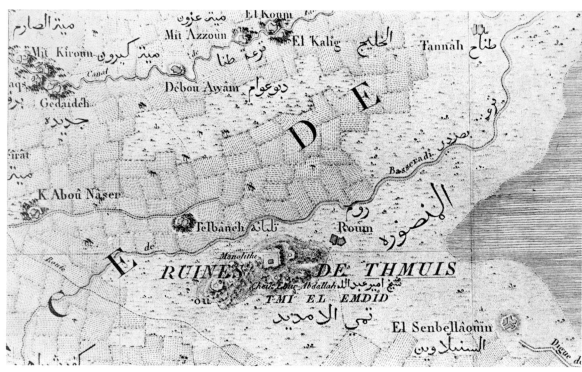

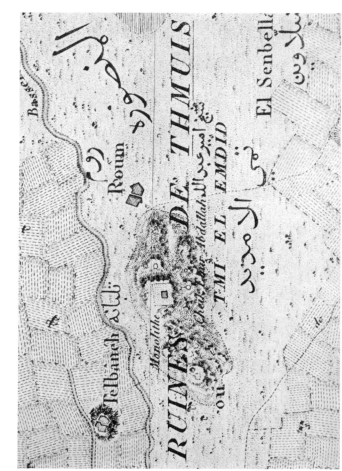

a   Detail of Plate 9-b   1800

b   Detail of Plate 9-b, rotated by 90°   1800

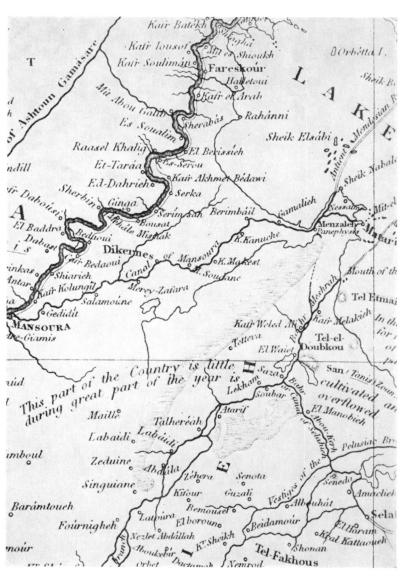

c   La Rochette, *Lower Egypt*   1802

d   Leake, *A Map of Egypt*   1818

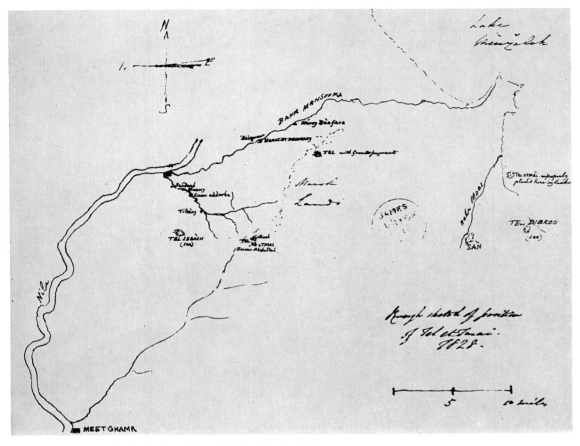

a   Burton, *Rough sketch of position of Tel et-Tmai. 1828*

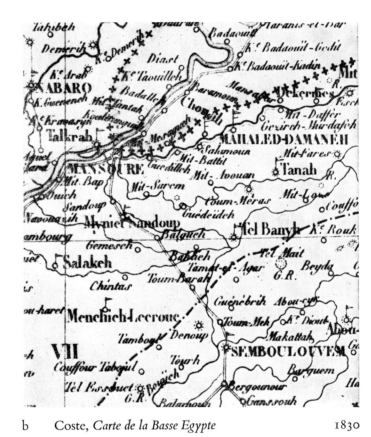

b   Coste, *Carte de la Basse Egypte*   1830

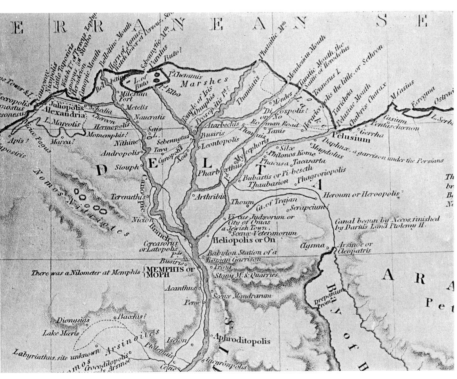

c   Long, *Ancient Egypt*   1831

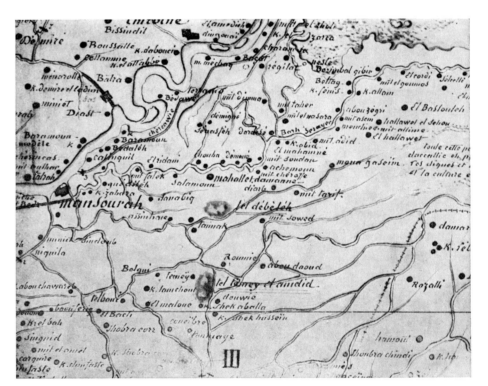

d   Linant de Bellefonds, *Carte de la Basse Egypte* (Ms.)   1841

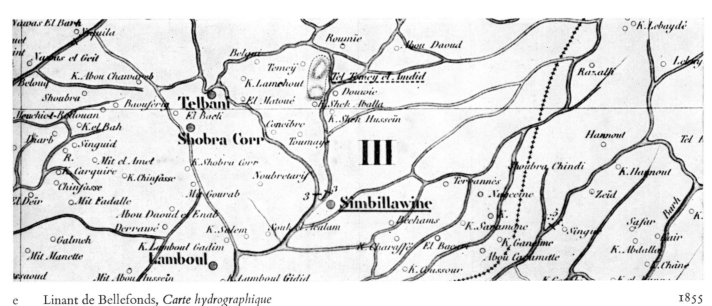

e   Linant de Bellefonds, *Carte hydrographique*   1855

PLATE 12   Maps of the Late 19th Century

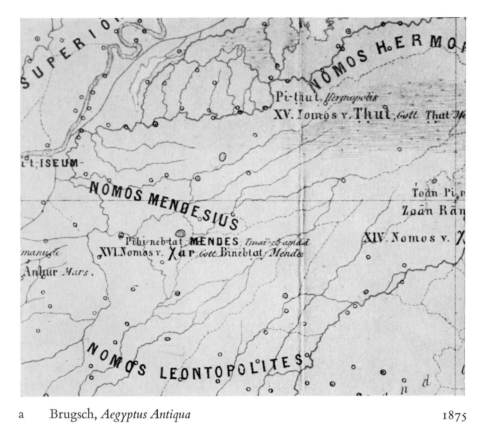

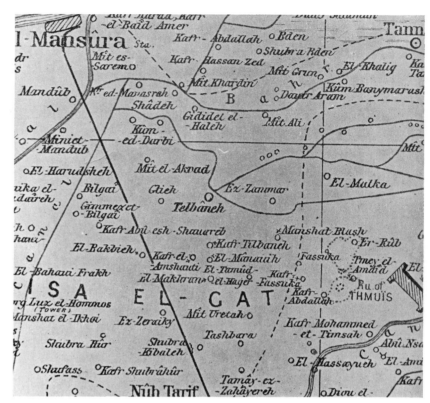

a   Brugsch, *Aegyptus Antiqua*   1875   b   British War Office, *Lower Egypt*   1882

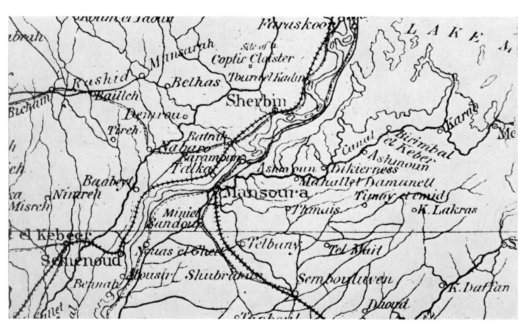

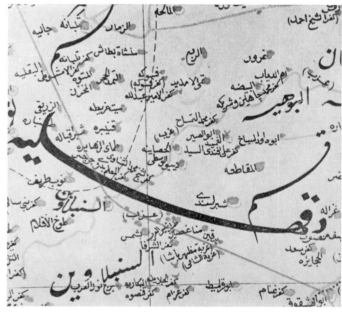

c   U. S. Army, *Lower Egypt*   1882   d   Mahmud el Falaki, *Sharq Tanta*   1888

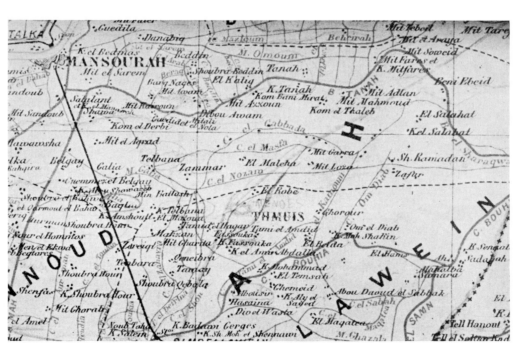

e   *Carte de la Basse Egypte*   1888

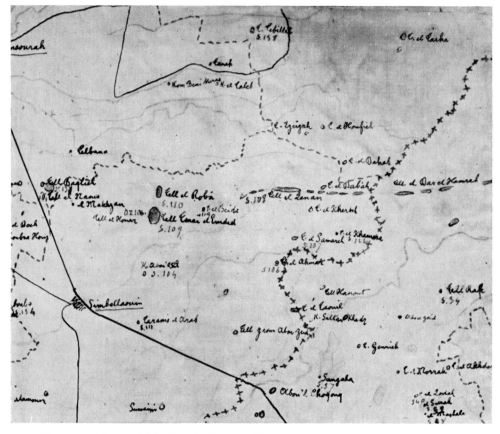

a   Daressy, *Atlas Archéologique de l'Egypte* (Ms.)

b   *Daqahlïya Province*   1896

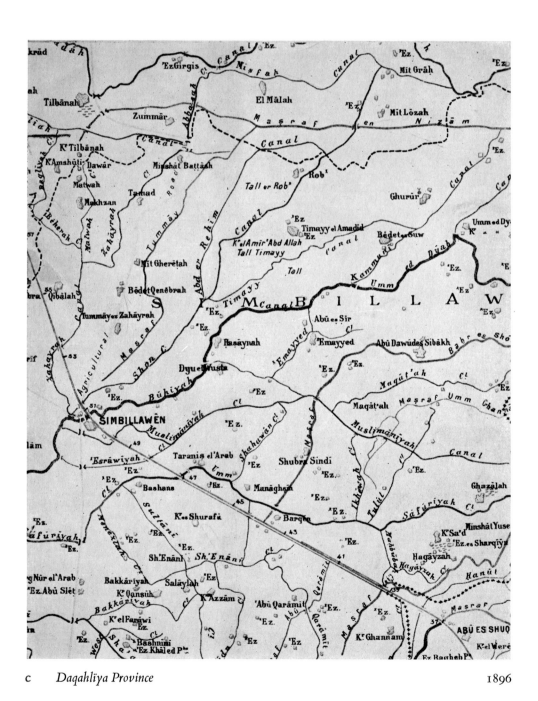

c   *Daqahlïya Province*   1896

d   Audébeau, Sauter and Colani, *Carte de la Basse Egypte*   1897

PLATE 14   Maps of the Early 20th Century (English and Arabic)

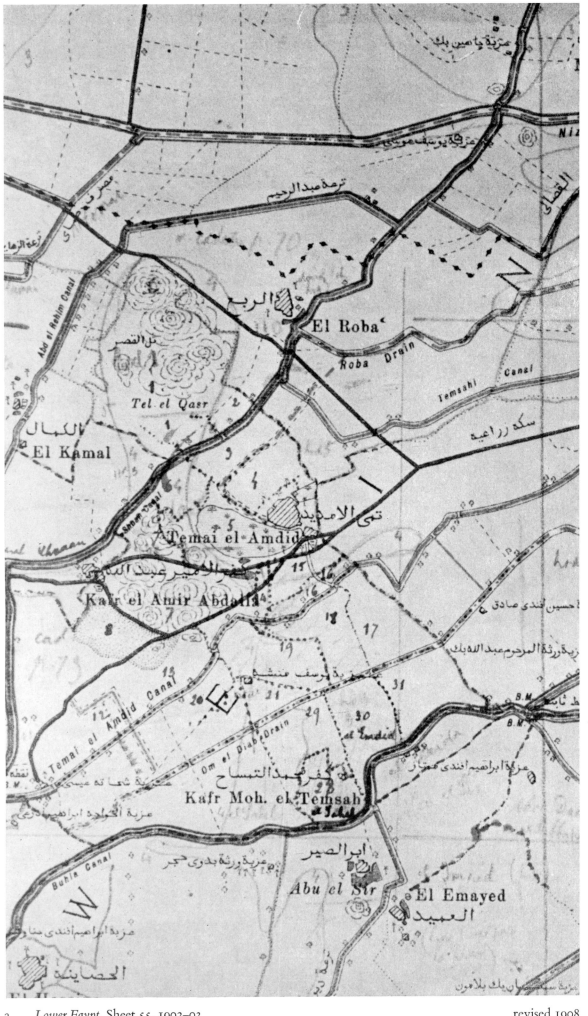

a   *Lower Egypt*, Sheet 55, 1902–03   revised 1908

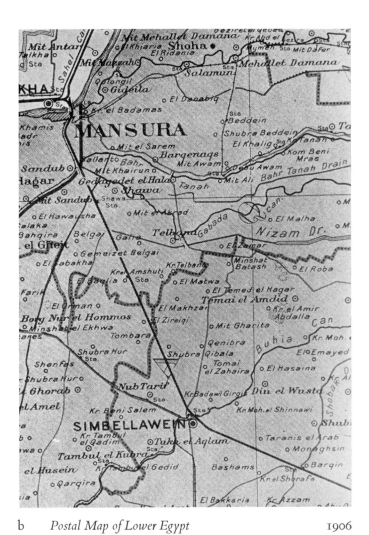

b   *Postal Map of Lower Egypt*   1906

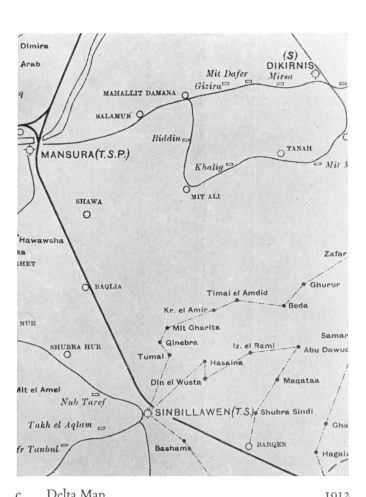

c   *Delta Map*   1912

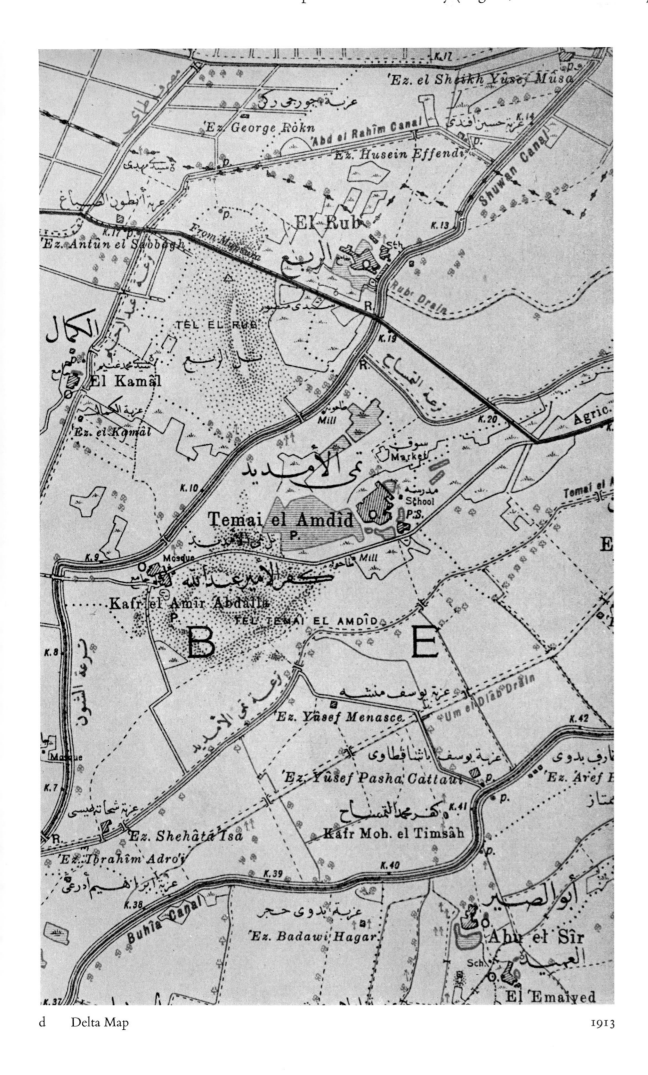

d   Delta Map   1913

e   Delta Map   1914

PLATE 15   Maps of the 20th Century (English, Arabic and German)

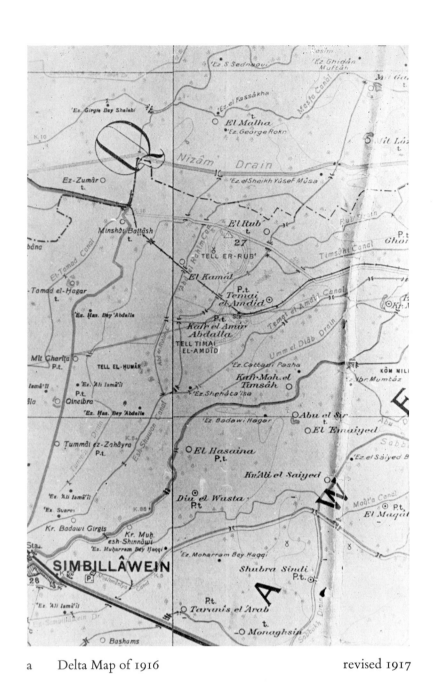

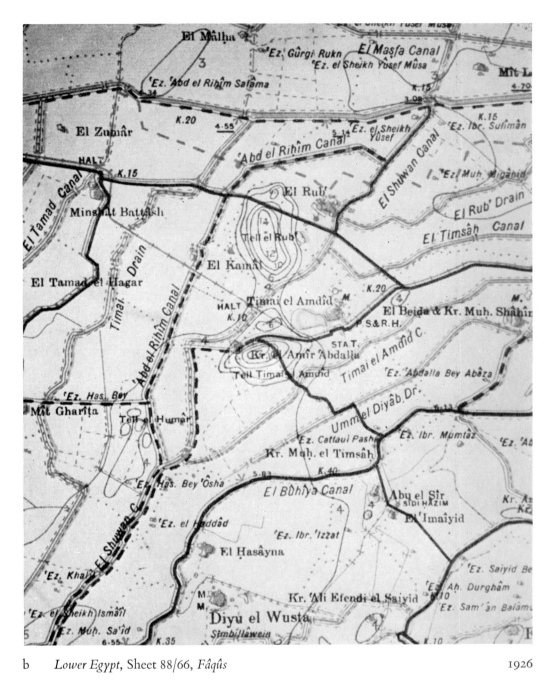

a   Delta Map of 1916   revised 1917   b   *Lower Egypt*, Sheet 88/66, *Fâqûs*   1926

c   *Lower Egypt*, Sheet 2, *Port Said*, 1933   second edition 1941

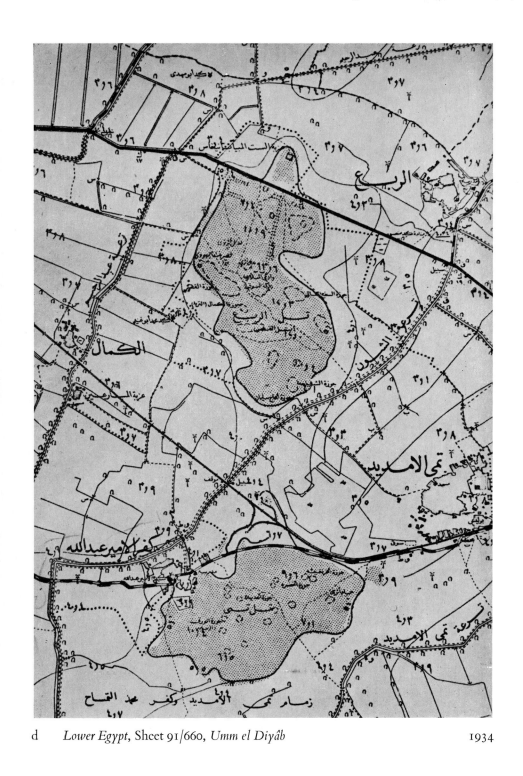

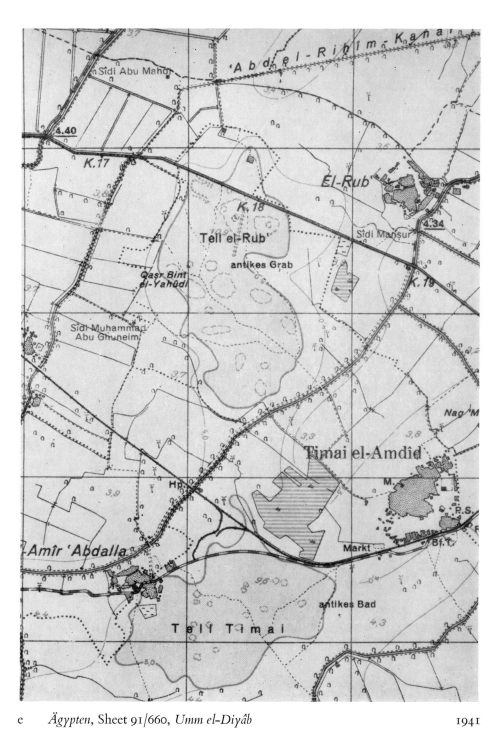

d   *Lower Egypt*, Sheet 91/660, *Umm el Diyâb*   1934   e   *Ägypten*, Sheet 91/660, *Umm el-Diyâb*   1941

PLATE 16   Recent Maps

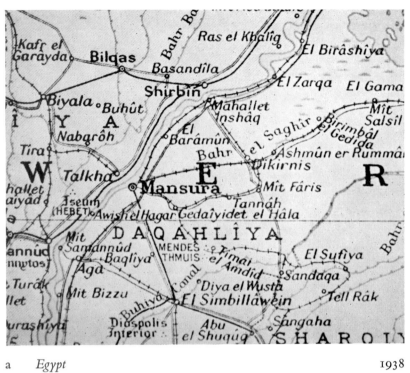

a   *Egypt*   1938

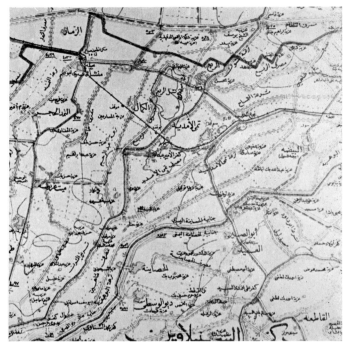

b   *Sharq Tanta*   1951

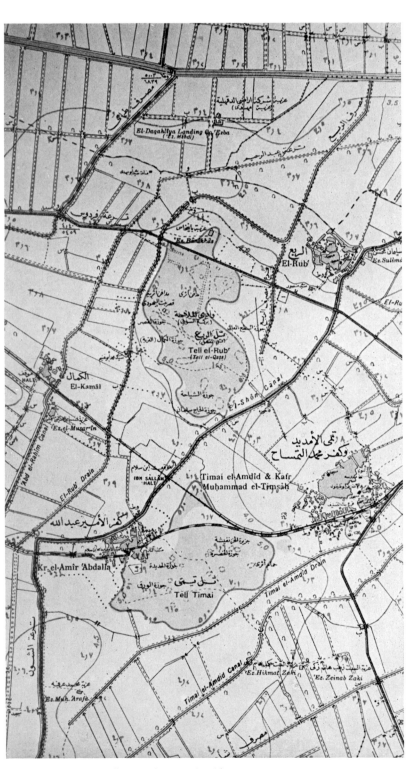

c   *Lower Egypt*, Sheet 91/660, *Tâg el 'Izz*   1952

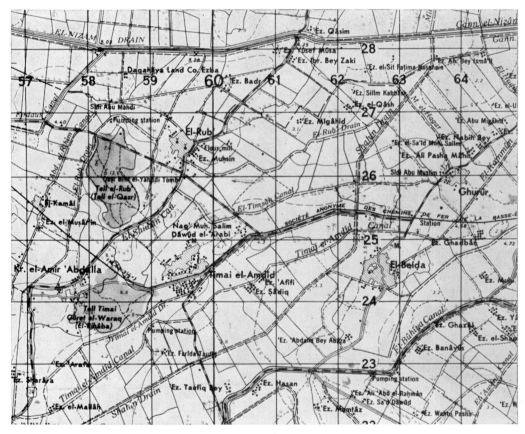

d   U.S. Army, *Egypt*, Sheet 5686 IV, *Tell Râk*   1958

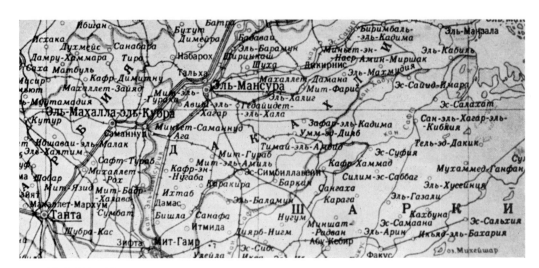

e   U.S.S.R., *Egypt*   1965

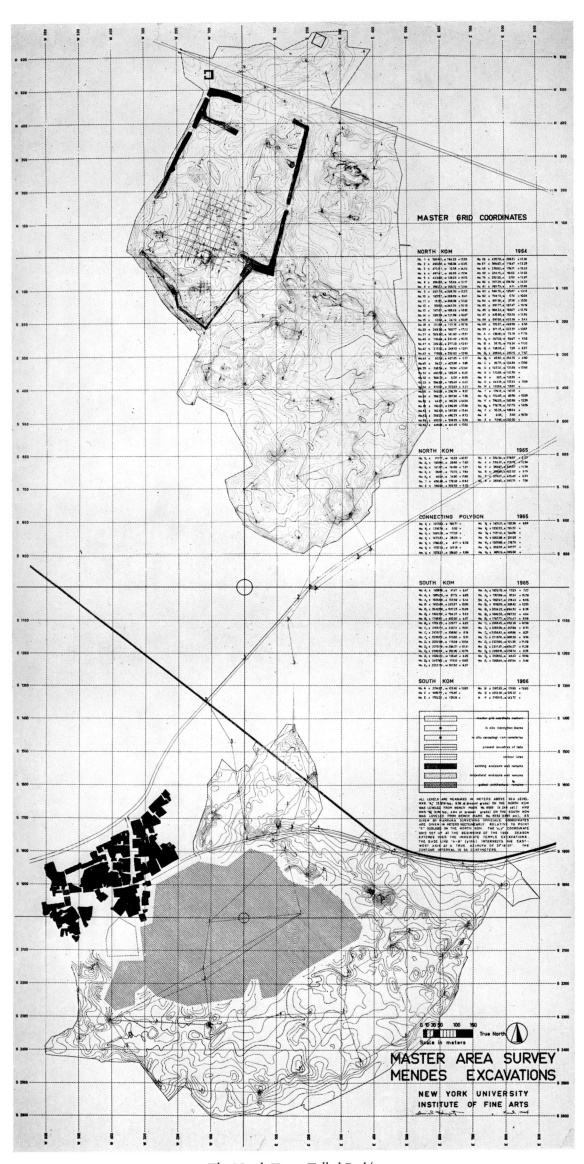

The North Kom: Tell el Rub‘a
The South Kom: Tell Timai

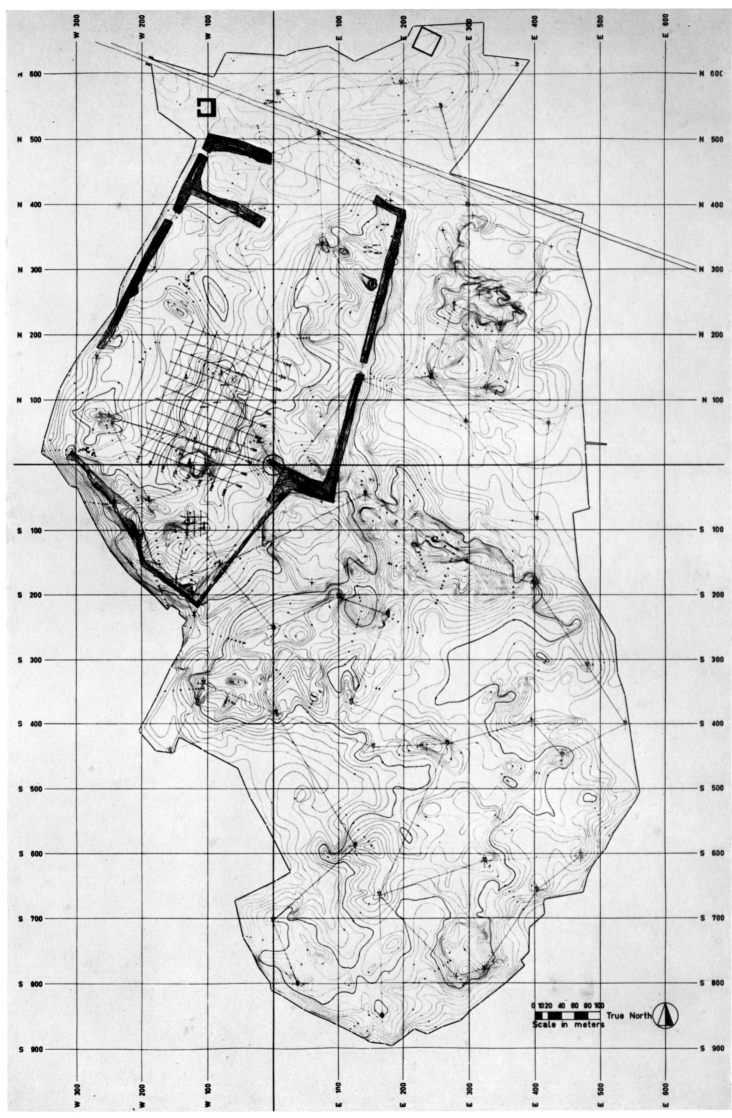

The North Kom

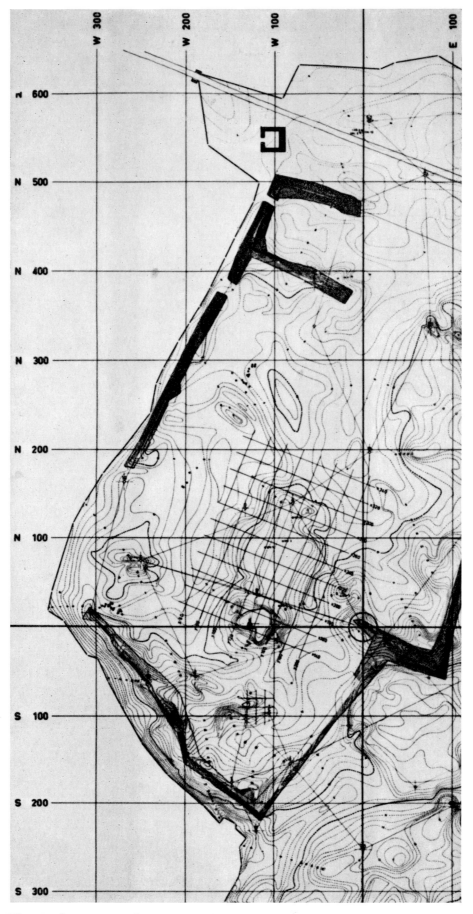

The North Kom: Northwestern Section, S 300 – E 300

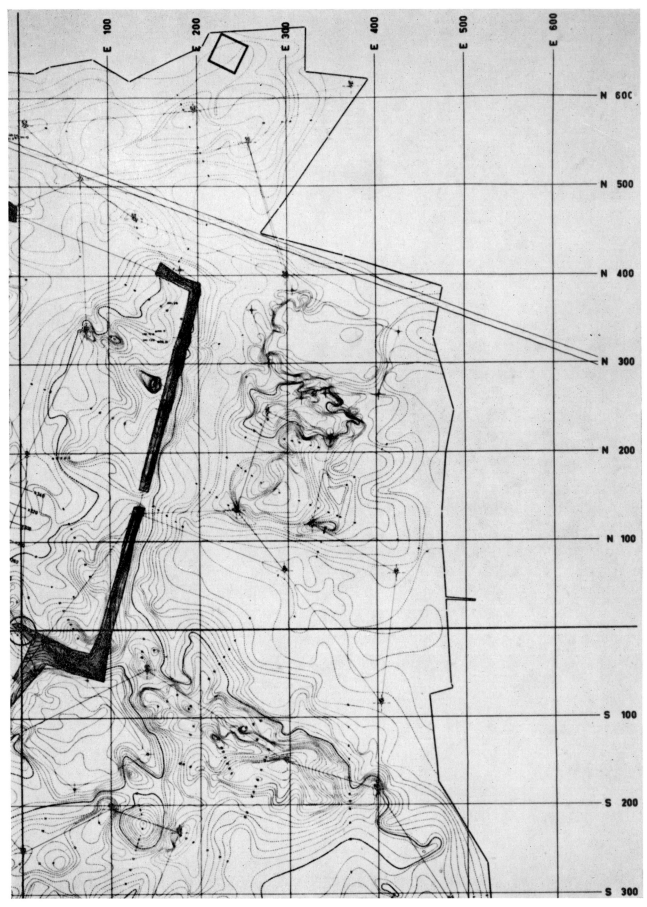

The North Kom: Northeastern Section, N 670 – S 300, WE 00 – E 525

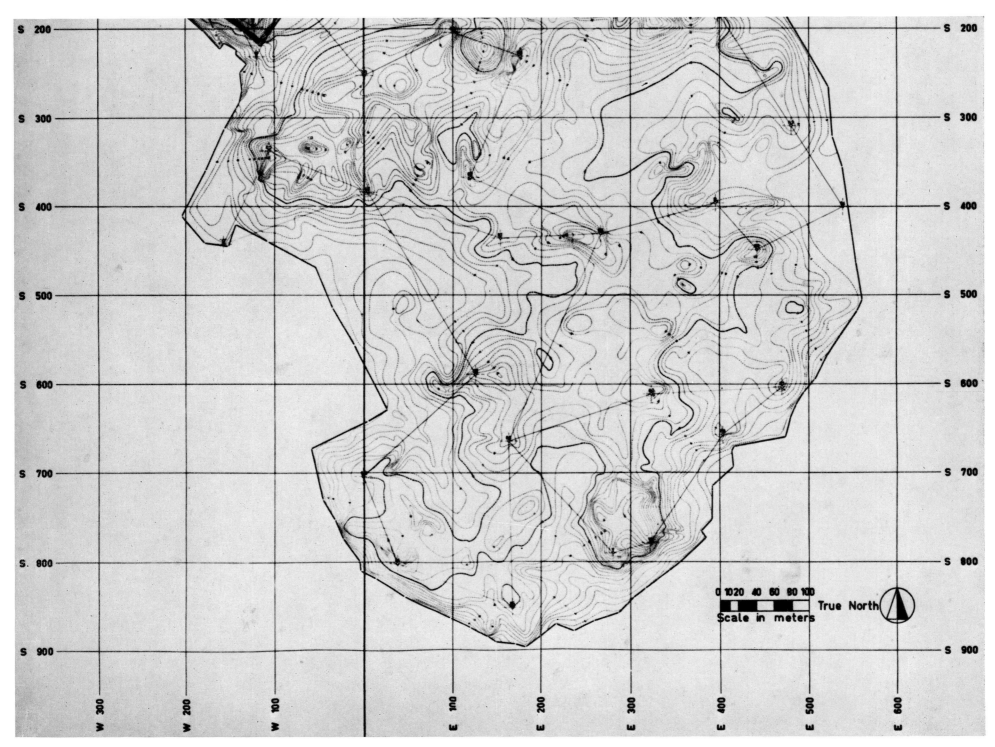

The North Kom: Southern Section, S 200 – 900, W 205 – E 565

PLATE 22   Tell Timai:

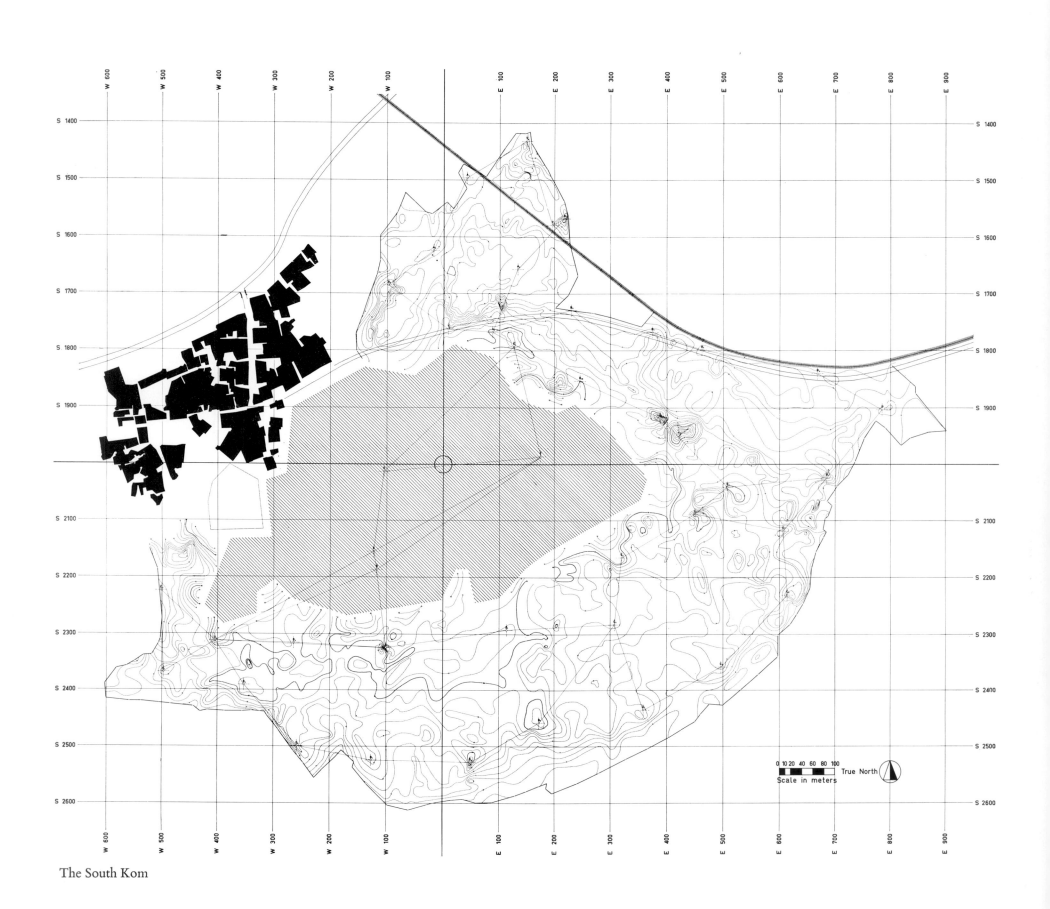

The South Kom

The South Kom: Northwestern Section, W 610 – E 100, S 1460 – 2200, with the Village of Kafr el Amir

PLATE 24

Tell Timai

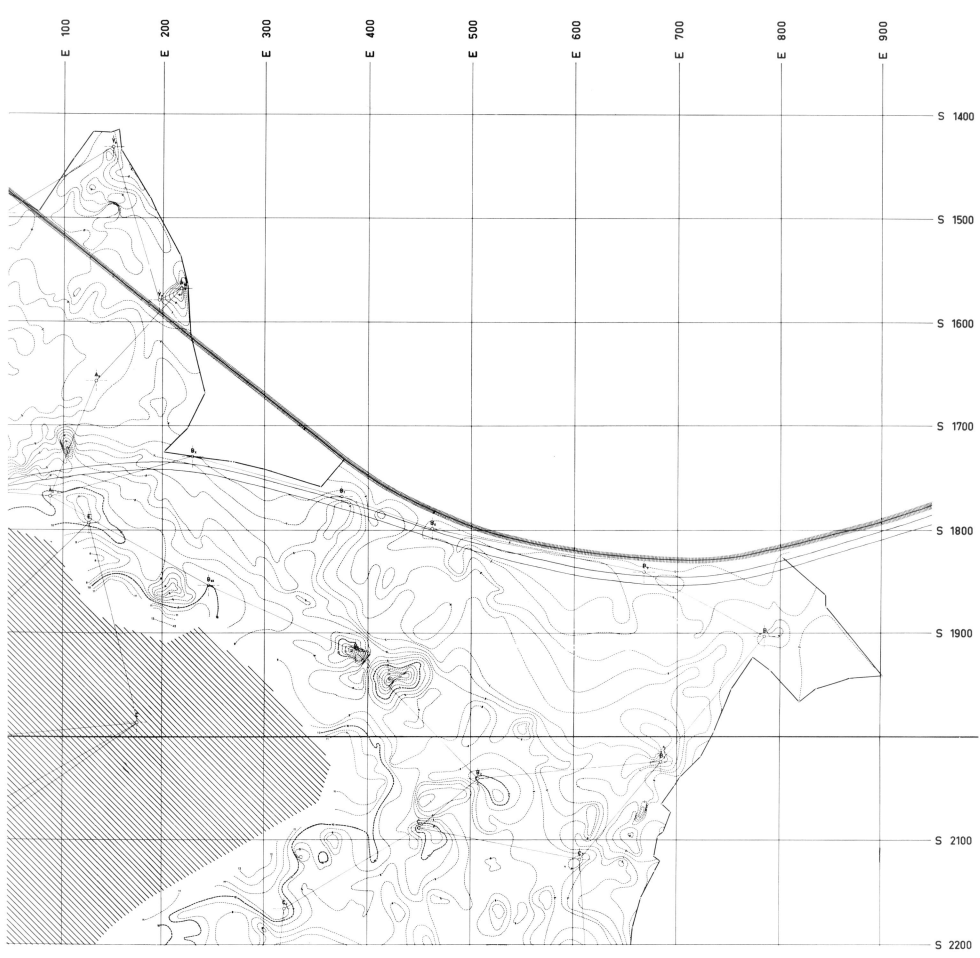

The South Kom: Northeastern Section, E 50 – E 900, S 1420 – 2200

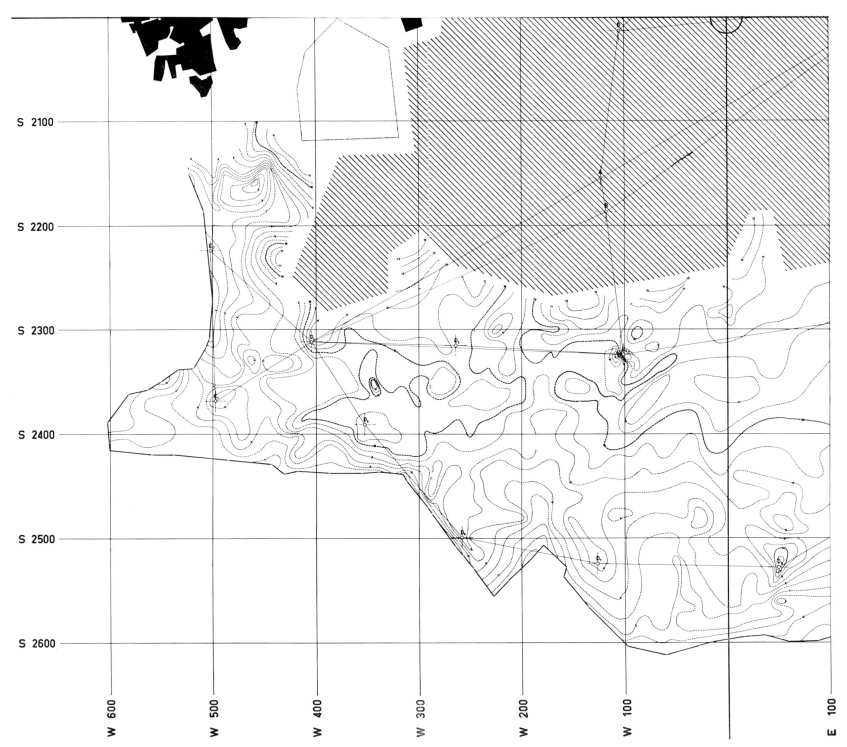

S 2100

S 2200

S 2300

S 2400

S 2500

S 2600

W 600   W 500   W 400   W 300   W 200   W 100   E 100

The South Kom: Southwestern Section, S 2000 – 2630, W 600 – E 100

Plate 26   Tell Timai

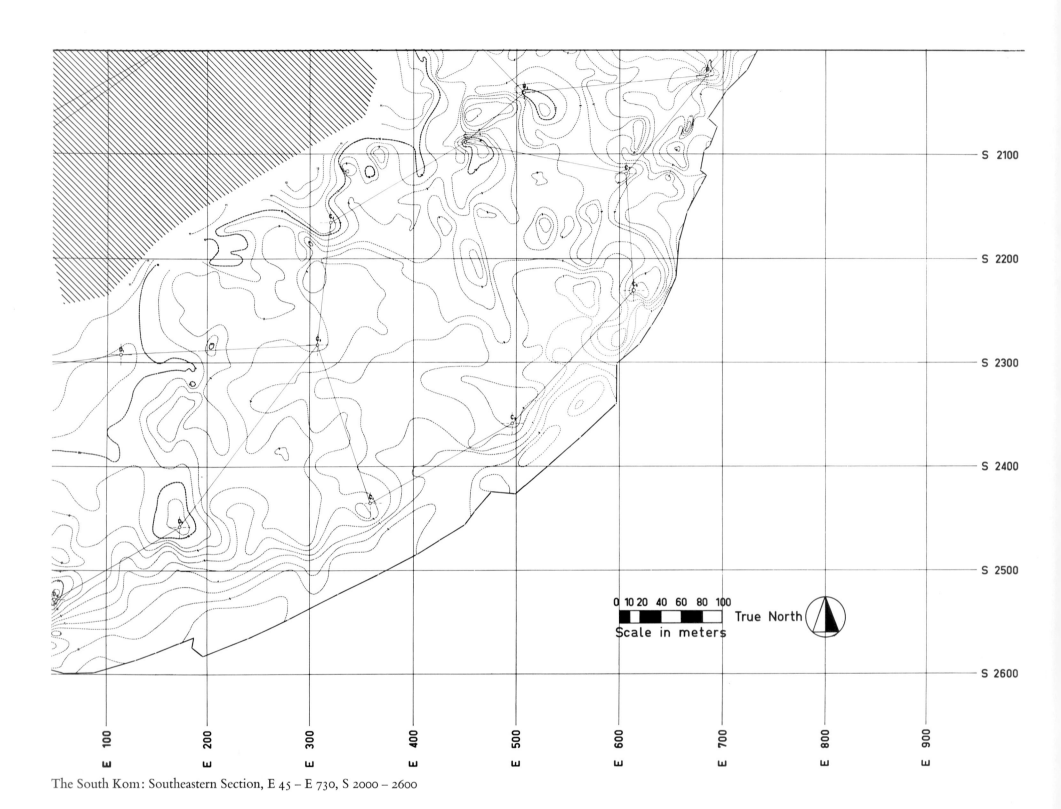

The South Kom: Southeastern Section, E 45 – E 730, S 2000 – 2600

a   Highest Elevation (on right) at South End of East Enclosure Wall (S 50 – E 60; Plate 19)

b   Vegetation at Southeastern Edge of Tell el Rub'a and in the Background the Houses of Timai el Amdid (E 340 – S 780; Plate 21)

c   *Safsoof* amidst Ram Sarcophagi

d   *Aqool* [This photograph was not taken at Mendes.]

e   Landform East of Tell el Rub'a, Taken from East of the Farm of Mansur el Arabi, Looking East

PLATE 28   Tell el Rub'a: Air View After the Excavation of 1966

a　　Part of West Enclosure Wall (with the opening at N 380 – W 160; Plate 19)

b　　Inside West Enclosure Wall, Looking North toward Northwestern Corner of Wall (from N 180 – W 200; Plate 19)

c　　From Northwestern Corner of Wall, Looking South, toward the Great Naos

d　　From Perpendicular Extension of West Wall (N 390 – W 30; Plate 19), Looking toward Northwestern Corner of Wall

PLATE 30   Tell el Rub'a: The Great Naos

a   Rise of the Temple Area, from Northnortheast

b   Before Excavation, from Northnortheast

c   Before Excavation, from Eastnortheast

e   Before Excavation, Temple Area with Stone Chips and Blocks, from Northnortheast

d   Before Excavation, from the East, Looking out over the Delta

a   Tomb of Tety-ishetef (6), from the North

b   Building Remains North of Temple Area (N 240 – W 140; Plate 19), Looking North. In Background, Left, Northern Group of Ram Sarcophagi and Northwestern Corner of Enclosure Wall

c   Ram Sarcophagi, Southern Group (N 20 – W 280; Plate 19), Looking West

d   Ram Sarcophagi, Northern Group (N 275 – W 135; Plate 19), Looking South

PLATE 32   Tell el Rub'a: Inside East Enclosure Wall

a   The Wall, from Highest Preserved Portion of Temple Precinct, Looking Northeast. In Background, Left, the *Ezbah* (N 640 – E 230; Plate 20)

b   Opening in Middle of Wall (N 150 – E 155; Plate 20), Looking Southeast

c   Decorated Granite Blocks (**11-14**) near Northeastern Corner of Wall (N 345 – E 160; Plate 20), Looking Southeast

d   Giant Sarcophagus (N 40 – E 60; Plate 20), Looking Northwest

a   Building Remains (S 350 – W 100; Plate 21), South of Great Naos, Looking Southwest

b   Mound East of Southern Tip (S 790 – E 330; Plates 21 and 35-c), Looking Northwest

c   Northern Tip, Looking Northeast toward the *Ezbah* (N 640 – E 230; Plate 20). At left a Portion of North Enclosure Wall (N 480 – W 20; Plate 19)

d   Blocks **8-10** (*Mendes* II, Plate 10 a–c) at North Side of Road (N 555 – W 5; Plate 19), Looking North

a   Tell el ʻIzam (N 270 – E 350; Plate 20), from the Road, Looking Southwest

b   Area South of Tell el ʻIzam, Looking Toward Southeast Corner of East Enclosure Wall

c   Building Remains Southeast of East Enclosure Wall (S 120 – E 250; Plate 20), Looking Southeast

d   Southern End of East Enclosure Wall (S 50 – E 90; Plate 19), Looking North across "Sacred Lake"

a   "Sacred Lake" from Southern End of East Enclosure Wall (S 50 – E 90; Plate 19), Looking Southsouthwest, toward Kafr el Amir Abdallah (Plate 17)

b   Building Remains South of Naos and Southwest of "Sacred Lake," Looking Southwest

c   Mound East of the Southern Tip of Tell el Rub'a (S 700 – E 300; Plates 21 and 33-b), Looking Southwest

PLATE 36   Tell Timai: Air View, After the Excavation of 1966

a   Panoramic View from Minaret in Village of Kafr el Amir Abdallah Sheikh Ibn es-Salam, Looking East (left) and South (right)

b   Central Section. Remains of Hellenistic Buildings, Looking Northwest toward Minaret of Kafr el Amir

c   Central Section. Ancient Street, Looking Southeast

a–b   Central Section. Building Remains with Windows, Second Storeys and Doorways

c–d   Northern Section (S 1630 – E 20; Plate 23). Foundations of Limestone Platform

a   Northern Section (S 1500 – E 40; Plate 23). Sarcophagus Fragments

b   Northern Section. Sphinx

c   Eastern Extension, Northern Part (Plate 24), Looking Eastnortheast, toward the
     Village of Timai el Amdid

d   South Area (Plate 26). Granite Capital

PLATE 40　　　　　　　　　　　　　　Tell Timai

a　　Southeastern Quarter (Plate 26). House Ruins

b　　South Area (S 2100–2600 – E 350, W 100; Plates 25, 26), with Remains of Granite Columns, Looking Westnorthwest. At Right, in the Distance, the Minaret of Kafr el Amir

c　　Panoramic View from Minaret of Kafr el Amir, Looking South (left) and Southwest (right)

INDEXES

Indexes

ORGANIZATIONS

GEOGRAPHICAL AND GEOLOGICAL TERMS

Addenda and Errata to *Mendes* II

Since, unfortunately, the publishers who originally intended to bring out both *Mendes* I and *Mendes* II decided to tackle the infinitely more complex second volume first, it contains a deplorably large number of omissions and errors for which we, the Editors, are only partly responsible.

P. ix
> Plate 12-c: for "Plate 5-a" read "Plate 4-a"

P. x
> Plate 17-e: for "Head. Back. . . ." read "Back. . ."
> Plate 17-f: for "Threequarter view" read "Head, three-quarter view"

P. xii
> Plate 28-c: for "**81, 4**" read **81, 4**"
> Plate 28: for "**81, 7**" read "f . . . **81, 7**"

P. xiii
> Plate 35-h: for "(*ME* 2M/35/35B/32/2.) read "*ME* 2M/35B/32/2)."
> Plate 37: for "**155**" read "e . . . **155**"
> Plate 39-a: for "**64-2179**" read "**64.2179**"
> Plate 39-b: for "Eton College." read "Eton College, Myers Museum 317."

P. 18
> In left margin, line 10, add: **112.**
> Note 1: for "See above" read "See below"
> Note 3: for "See above" read "See below"
> Note 15, last line, before square bracket, add: CG 53464-53540
> Note 20: for "*Mendes* I" read "*Mendes* I, Pp. vii, 16, 23, 24"
> Note 23, in left margin, last lines, add: **33**

P. 22
> With reference to Père Claude Sicard, S.J., one should consult S. Sauneron's report on his finding Sicard's papers in the Jesuit Library of Chantilly (*BIFAO* 74 [1974], pp. 221–223).

P. 33
> In right margin, line 8, add: **44-b** or **45**

P. 43
> In right margin, line 1, add: **44-b** or **45**

P. 92
> Lines 6-7: for "(see, above, P. 14, and below P. 184)." read "(see above, P. 14; below, P. 203 and Plate 29-e, -f, -g)."

P. 96
> In left margin, line 3, add: **1**

P. 97
> At bottom, end of line 1 of Note 1, add: "the"

P. 125
> Par. 2: The limestone block with cartouches of Apries can no longer be located in the mosque of the village of El Rub'a, which has been thoroughly restored since Naville's visit.
> Lines 7 & 8: The only "house of a Greek" near the site, which can be identified today, is the *ezbah* situated on the northern tip of Tell el Rub'a. Although ancient blocks without decoration can be found in buildings throughout the village, "the base of a kneeling statue" was not discovered on a visit in July, 1979.

P. 135
> Delete both illustrations; see Plate 2-b, -c

P. 141
> End of text, in right margin, add: **12** (Plate 11-a)

P. 142
> In left margin, add: **232**

P. 146
> Line 4: To first reference to *Mendes* I, add: "(P. 25, Pl. 38-c, -d);" to second reference, add: "(P. 24 and Note 7)."
> Line 6: Omit "(see below, P. 152)."

P. 152
> Line 7, for "annés" read "années"

P. 162
> In the margin before **1**, add: **2** or **5**

P. 168
> Line 1, for "Marcel" read "Marcelle"

P. 177
> In Note 3, line 3, for "ägyptischem" read "ägyptischen".

P. 179
> **226** in paragraph 3 refers to "A curious mold . . ." mentioned at the bottom of P. 216.

P. 180
> In Note 1, for " 'Le poison de Mendès' " read " 'Le nome du dauphin et du poisson de Mendès,' "

P. 181
> In Note 48, line 1, for "Heiroglyphic" read "Hieroglyphic"

P. 182
> At bottom, right, for "XVII" read "XVIII"

P. 183
> At top, right, for "XVIII, 6" read "XVIII, 16"
> For "Bresciani, III" read "Bresciani, *op. cit.* III, 3; XXI, 23", and delete third line, at middle, right column.

P. 191
> To **2**, line 5, for "The block also shows . . ." read "The inscription is preceded by . . ."
> A number of objects from Mendes are listed and described in G. Maspero, *Guide du visiteur du Musée de Boulaq* (1883), and in J. de Morgan, *Notice des principaux monuments du Musée de Gizeh* (1897). The latter has a site index where, on page 399 (s.v. Tell Tmaï), the objects can be located.

P. 192
> To **11**, add: While two sides of **11** are illustrated on Plate 10-d, -e, the third side is visible in *Mendes* I, on Plate 32-c, lower left.
> To **12**, add: "See Page 141 above and Pl. 11-a below."

P. 193
> To **19** add: *PM* IV (1934), p. 35
> To **20** and **21** add: *PM* IV (1934), p. 36

P. 194
> To **24** add: *PM* IV (1934), p. 37; Zivie, *Hermopolis*, pp. 245–46, Doc. 103
> To **25** add: Free-standing columns are also represented on the shrine of Saft el Henna, Cairo CG 70021: G. Roeder, *Naos* (1914), p.l 32 (tp. Nectanebo I), and Cairo TR $\frac{22|12}{20|2}$ (M. 1180), said to have come from "Ganag near Sulhagar," may also have been free-standing. Finally, Lauffray, in *Kêmi* 20 (1970), pp. 153–164, convincingly argues that the ten columns of the so-called Taharqo Kiosk at Karnak were always isolated and probably never supported architraves and a roof.

P. 195
> To **34**, add: De Meulenaere, in *LdÄ* II (1978), col. 932.

P. 196
> To **43**, add: Borchardt, *Statuen* (CGC) IV (1930), p. 122, pl. 172.

P. 197
> To **44-b**, add: See above, Pp. 33 and 43. As J. J. Clère, Janine Bourriau, and the Editors have long seen, this statue was made in the New Kingdom and bears a

Ramesside inscription on both sides, behind and below the Hathor emblem. The date given, "early Dynasty XXVI," applies to the back pillar inscription only, which obviously was added hundreds of years after the sculpture was made.
> To **45**, add: See above, Pp. 33 and 43. The name of the owner was Iahmes, now known from another fragmentary statue of him (5 M 34) found at Tell el Rub'a on 24 July 1977 and now in the Cairo Museum.
> To **47**, add: Borchardt, *Statuen* (CGC) III (1930), p. 64, pl. 135; *PM* IV (1934), p. 36.

P. 198
> To **55**, add: *PM* IV (1934), p. 37.

P. 199
> To **62**, add: Zivie, *Hermopolis*, pp. 157–58, Doc. 49.

P. 200
> To **68**, add: See above, Pp. 86–87.

P. 201
> To **80**, add: On a visit to Alexandria in July, 1979, it was found that Alexandria nos. 23032–23043 (except for the first one) were all limestone and marble fragments not listed in *Mendes* II. The provenances given were: "Direction Générale, Tell Basta, Thmouis" or "Thmouis-Zagazig" or "Tell Basta-Thmouis."
> To **81**, add: *PM* IV (1934), p. 37.
> To **82**, line 7, end: for "*JEA* 17" read "*JEA* 47". Last line, add: *PM* IV (1934), p. 36; G. Poethke, in *LdÄ* I (1975), col. 895.
> To **82**, add: H. Jucker, "Römische Herrscherbildnisse aus Ägypten," *Aufstieg und Niedergang der Römischen Welt* 12, Part II (1979), p. 55, pl. LVI:51.

P. 203
> To **97**, add: Aubert, *Statuettes*, p. 244.
> At **100**, delete "None." and add: Aubert, *op. cit.*, pp. 255, 259, figs. 155–156. Another shawabti of this man is in Brooklyn (acc.no. 05.401); others are in Amsterdam, Berlin, London, Leiden (Schneider, *Shabtis* II, pp. 184–85, pl. 126; III, pl. 61), Stockholm (Peterson, in *Medelhavsmuseet Bulletin* 12 [1977], pp. 20–21, no. 7; others, attributed to Mendes, on pp. 21–22), and elsewhere. Two other shawabtis, of Ba-ankh and Wah-ib-ra, may also have come from Mendes (Schneider, *Shabtis* II, pp. 168–69, 162).

P. 204
> Note 7: for "1890)," read "1890,"
> Note 8, line 2: for "48" read **48**

P. 205
> To **108**, add: *PM* IV (1934), p. 35.
> To **109** add: G. Posener, "Les douanes de la Méditerranée dans l'Egypte saïte," *Revue de Philologie* XXI, 2 (1947), p. 125, n. 3, and D. Meeks, "Les donations aux temples dans l'Egypte du Ier millénaire avant J.-C.," *Orientalia Lovaniensia Analecta* 6 (1979), p. 678.

P. 206
> To **111**, add: G. Poethke, in *LdÄ* I (1975), col. 451; D. Meeks, *op. cit.* II (1978), col. 1010.
> To **112**, add: "See also P. 18 above."

P. 207

    Before **123**, add: A major study of the libation tables has now been published as a doctoral dissertation of December, 1978, by Vivian A. Hibbs. It is entitled, *The Mendes Maze: a Libation Table for the Genius of the Inundation of the Nile* (*II–III A.D.*), available in microfilm from University Microfilms, P. O. Box 1346, Ann Arbor, Michigan 48108.

P. 212

    Note 13, add: For the circumstances of finding some of the mosaics, see F. Rattigan, *Diversions of a Diplomat* (London, 1924), pp. 100–102.

P. 213

    With reference to **162**, Cairo JE 40302, the location of the sarcophagus of Semekh-sen was not known until recently, when it was found under a temporary number in a locked room in the Cairo Museum.

P. 214

    To **168**, add to Bibliography: See also P. 18, n. 15, above.

P. 216

    For "see above, P. 00" read "see P. 17, paragraph 5."

P. 217

    To **232**, add: See also P. 142.

    After **233-234**, before *Notes*, add:

    Note Two: Two inscribed vases were omitted from the *List of Objects:* one in Cairo, the other in Berlin.

    Cairo CG 16037 Alabaster vase of Tety, Dynasty VI; inscribed, "Beloved of the Ram of Mendes . . ." Bibliography: A. Mariette, *Catalogue général des monuments d'Abydos* (Paris, 1880), p. 573, no. 1464; *PM* V, p. 73; C. Soghor, in *JARCE* 6 (1967), p. 31 and note 41. The objects which Mariette lists at the end of the *Catalogue* may not have been found at Abydos, and this vase might well have come from Mendes.

Berlin 19/67 Alabaster vase with the Horus name of Tety. Bibliography: *Ägyptisches Museum Berlin* (1967), p. 28, no. 239, illus.; C. Soghor, in *JARCE* 6 (1967), p. 31 and note 42.

Note 21, line 2: for "Mendes," read "Mendes."

P. 241

    At top: for "195, Note 7" read "204, Note 7."

    New objects listed above but not included in *Mendes* II (Pp. 240–243) are as follows:

	related to Object	Page
Alexandria 23033–23043	**80**	201
Berlin 19/67	—	217, Note 2
Brooklyn 05.401	**100**	213
Cairo CG 16037	—	217, Note 2
CG 53464–53540	—	18, N. 15
CG 70021	**25**	194
TR $\frac{22|12}{20|2}$	**25**	194

Plate 1-b

    For ". . . looking West." read ". . . looking East."

Plate 7-f

    For "capital" read "pedestal base"

Plate 8-b, -c, -d

    At right, add: **2**

    Plate 8-d should be to the left of 8-b on the south face of the block. The columnar divider between them has been omitted. Plate 8-c forms the east face and represents the right side of the block. The *t3wj* group, cut off at the edge, is in fact completely preserved.

Plate 18

    44 a-c shows **44-b** on the *List of Objects*

Plate 35-g

    Reverse illustration upside down.

Additional Bibliography and Abbreviations to *Mendes* II

Aubert, *Statuettes*   J.-F. and L. Aubert, *Statuettes égyptiennes, chaouabtis, ouchebtis* (Paris, 1974).

BdE   *Bibliothèque d'Etude*

M. Bietak, *Tell el-Dab'a* II (Vienna, 1975), passim. and figs. 38–43.

B. V. Bothmer, "Excavations at Mendes, 1964," *AJA* 69 (1965), p. 165.

K. Briggs, "A Season at Mendes," *IFA News* (New York) 24 (1977–78), p. 5.

Encyclopedia International 6 (New York, 1970), pl. 8.

M. B. Freeman, *Finding out about the Past* (New York, 1967), pp. 66–67 (northern group of rams' coffins).

K. B. Gödecken, in *Ägyptologische Abhandlungen* 29 (1976), pp. 194, 281, n. 130; 378, n. 36.

Grimm, *Kunst*   G. Grimm, *Kunst der Ptolemäer- und Römerzeit im Ägyptischen Museum Kairo* (Mainz, 1975).

D. Hansen, "Mendes 1964," *JARCE* 4 (1965), pp. 31–37, pls. XVI–XXI.

———, "Excavation of a Stratified Pharaonic Site in the Egyptian Delta at Mendes, 1966 Season," *NARCE* 61 (March, 1967), pp. 9–13.

———, "The Excavations at Tell el Rub'a," *JARCE* 6 (1967), pp. 5–16, pls. I–XV.

W. Helck and E. Otto (Eds.), *Lexikon der Ägyptologie* I (1976), cols. 188, 336, 1048 (fig. 2, map), 1103, 1189, 1263.

———, II (1978), cols. 192–93, 229, 231, 236, 400, 408, 643, 666, 692, 760, 793, 822, 931–32, 1006, 1015, 1042–43, 1117.

R. K. Holz, "Man-made Landforms in the Nile Delta," *The Geographical Review* 59 (1969), pp. 253–59, figs. 1–12.

L. Kákosy, "Prophecies of Ram Gods," *Acta Orientalia* (Budapest) 19 (1966), pp. 343, 351, nn. 70, 71; 354 and nn. 86, 88, 355 and n. 89.

S. Kambitsis, in *CdE* 51 (1976), pp. 130–140.

———, in *BIFAO* 76 (1976), pp. 225–230.

LdÄ   *Lexikon der Ägyptologie* (Wiesbaden).

J. Leclant, "Fouilles et travaux en Egypte et au Soudan," *Orientalia* 34 (1965), pp. 179–80, pl. XXV;
    35 (1966) pp. 133–34, pls. II–III, figs. 2–4;
    36 (1967), p. 184;
    37 (1968), pp. 97–98, pls. XI–XII, figs. 3–5;
    45 (1976), p. 279;
    46 (1977), p. 236;
    47 (1978), p. 269.
    48 (1979), pp. 346–7, pls. II–III

J. Mazuel, *L'oeuvre géographique de Linant de Bellefonds* (Cairo, 1937).

NARCE   *American Research Center in Egypt, Inc., Newsletter.*

E. Ochsenschlager, "The Excavations at Thmuis," *JARCE* 6 (1967), pp. 32–51, pls. XIX–XXI.

———, "The *Plemochoe*, A Vessel from Thmuis," *JARCE* 7 (1968), pp. 55–71, pl. I, figs. 1–5.

———, "The Cosmic Significance of the *Plemochoe*," *History of Religions* 9 (1970), pp. 316–36.

——— "Excavation of the Graeco-Roman City Thmuis in the Nile Delta," *Annales Archéologiques Arabes Syriennes* 21 (1971), pp. 185–91, ill.

B. Peterson, "Gesicht und Kunststil . . ." *Bulletin of the Medelhavsmuseet* 12 (1977), pp. 20–22, illus. [shawabtis].

I. Powell, "Important Discoveries in the Nile Delta," *Arab Observer* 321 (1966), pp. 40–43, ill.

F. Rattigan, *Diversions of a Diplomat* (London, 1924), pp. 100–102.

H. D. Schneider, *Shabtis* I–III (Leiden, 1977).

C. L. Soghor, "Inscriptions from Tell el Rub'a," *JARCE* 6 (1967), pp. 16–32, pls. XVI–XVIII.

G. R. H. Wright, "Tell el-Yehūdīyah and the Glacis," *Zeitschrift des Deutschen Palästina-Vereins* 84 (1968), pp. 13–16, pls. 6–8.

J. Weinstein, *Foundation Deposits in Ancient Egypt* (Ph.D. diss., U. of Pa., 1973), pp. 195–96, 336–37.

Zivie, *Hermopolis*   A.-P. Zivie, *Hermopolis et le nome de l'Ibis* (Cairo, 1971) = *BdE* 66 (1971).